A Passion For
Patterned Paper

More than 50 fresh and clever techniques
for scrapbooking

by Brandi Ginn & Pam Klassen

**MEMORY
MAKERS
BOOKS**

Memory Makers Books

Authors Brandi Ginn, Pam Klassen

Senior Editor MaryJo Regier

Art Director Nick Nyffeler

Graphic Designers Jordan Kinney, Robin Rozum

Art Acquisitions Editor Janetta Abucejo Wieneke

Photographer Ken Trujillo

Contributing Photographers Lizzy Creazzo, Brenda Martinez, Jennifer Reeves

Contributing Memory Makers Masters Jenn Brookover, Kelli Noto, Shannon Taylor

Editorial Support Jodi Amidei, Karen Cain, Emily Curry Hitchingham, Lydia Rueger, Dena Twinem

Memory Makers® A Passion for Patterned Paper

Published by Memory Makers Books, an imprint of F+W Publications, Inc.

12365 Huron Street, Suite 500, Denver, CO 80234

Phone 1-800-254-9124

First edition. Printed in the United States.

09 08 07 06 05   5 4 3 2 1

Library of Congress Cataloging-in-Publication Data

Ginn, Brandi
    A passion for patterned paper : more than 50 fresh and clever techniques for
scrapbooking / by Brandi Ginn & Pam Klassen.– 1st ed.
        p. cm.
    Includes index.
    ISBN 1-892127-51-2
        1. Photograph albums. 2. Photographs–Conservation and restoration. 3. Scrapbooks. 4.
Paper work. I. Klassen. Pam. II. Title.

TR465.G56 2005
745.593--dc22

                                                                2005041556

Distributed to trade and art markets by

F+W Publications, Inc.

4700 East Galbraith Road, Cincinnati, OH 45236

Phone 1-800-289-0963

ISBN 1-892127-51-2

Memory Makers Books is the home of *Memory Makers*, the scrapbook magazine dedicated to educating and inspiring scrapbookers.
To subscribe, or for more information, call 1-800-366-6465. Visit us on the Internet at www.memorymakersmagazine.com.

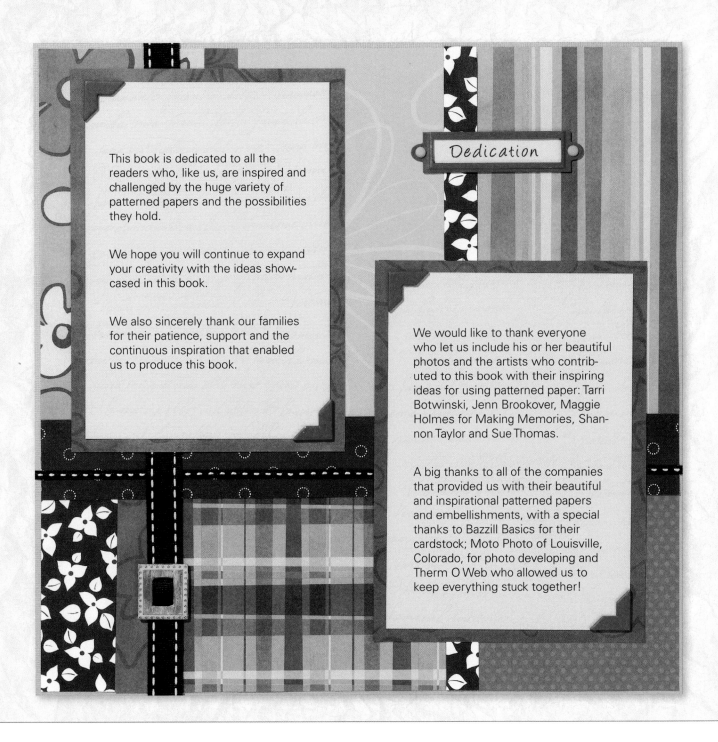

This book is dedicated to all the readers who, like us, are inspired and challenged by the huge variety of patterned papers and the possibilities they hold.

We hope you will continue to expand your creativity with the ideas showcased in this book.

We also sincerely thank our families for their patience, support and the continuous inspiration that enabled us to produce this book.

Dedication

We would like to thank everyone who let us include his or her beautiful photos and the artists who contributed to this book with their inspiring ideas for using patterned paper: Tarri Botwinski, Jenn Brookover, Maggie Holmes for Making Memories, Shannon Taylor and Sue Thomas.

A big thanks to all of the companies that provided us with their beautiful and inspirational patterned papers and embellishments, with a special thanks to Bazzill Basics for their cardstock; Moto Photo of Louisville, Colorado, for photo developing and Therm O Web who allowed us to keep everything stuck together!

Table of Contents

INTRODUCTION 7   COLOR 8   COLOR VALUE 9   PATTERN 10   SCALE 11   PLACEMENT 12   STORAGE 13

Babies 14-19

Graphic-Inspired Ideas 38-43

Children 26-31

Birthdays 20-25

Heritage 44-49

Feminine Ideas 32-37

Nature 62-67

Holidays & Seasons 50-55

Travel 80-85

School & Sports 68-73

Masculine Ideas 56-61

Vintage & Retro 86-91

Sentiments 74-79

PATTERNS 92

ADDITIONAL INSTRUCTIONS
& CREDITS 92-93

SOURCES 93-94

ABOUT THE AUTHORS 95

INDEX 96

And the fruit will outdo what the flowers have promised.

Francois de Malherbe

Jacquelyn & Amanda 2004

"I find myself now drawn to pulling more patterns into everyday life...my clothes, my home, my children." -Brandi

"Trying dozens of combinations before the perfect one strikes me is the process that personalizes each project." -Pam

Introduction

The appeal of patterned paper is universal. Each pattern can inspire our passion and evoke a feeling. They can help us showcase the celebration of a baby or birthday, the busy activities of a child or school day, relive the memories of our travels and preserve the treasure of our heritage. We automatically reach out to a pattern that touches us.

We have been inspired countless times to use patterned paper in our own projects. They allow us to create a variety of compositions and designs while remaining true to our individual style. We're drawn to their color, theme, design and creative potential. As career scrapbook designers who have mixed almost every pattern possible, we know that all the patterns out there can be overwhelming and intimidating. From tried-and-true combinations to incorporating various styles of paper with cutting-edge techniques, there are seemingly endless ways to use patterned paper.

Throughout our own design experiences, we have collected ideas and information for combining and assembling a wide array of patterned paper. Each chapter of this book includes a theme category to help utilize your papers in different ways—as embellishments, accents and backgrounds—with ways to use monochromatic papers and coordinating products. We'll also teach you how to alter papers and create your own patterns. We've used traditional products—like chalk and die cuts—as well as paint, Pattern Builder, walnut ink and aging mediums to help you make the most of your patterned-paper creations.

We hope that the ideas throughout this book will motivate and teach you how to use your patterned paper to its fullest potential while enhancing your creativity. If you love patterned paper, you will surely be inspired by the many examples presented in this book.

Brandi Pam

Brandi Ginn and Pam Klassen
Authors
Memory Makers A Passion for Patterned Paper

Color

We are constantly influenced by the colors around us. Whether intentionally or subconsciously, color influences the way we feel about our surroundings. With color playing such an important role in the page-design process, learning how to effectively use it should be a priority. When properly used, a color wheel can create the perfect color blends for any design. It creates combinations that are well-balanced and complementary to each other.

Primary colors are those that cannot be mixed from other colors—red, yellow, and blue. In their purest form they are bright, bold and expressive. When white is added to the pure color it creates a tint. Tones are created when gray is mixed with the pure color and shades are created when black is added.

In this layout more subtle shades of green, red, yellow and blue are used to create the design. Using shades of color rather than the purest form creates a more subdued tone.

Warm & Cool Color

Not only do colors have various intensities, they also have temperatures. Colors can be warm or cool with undertones from each temperature. For example, reds can be found to have a cool blue undertone or a warm orange undertone. If each undertone were used within the same design they would clash. Using color families with the same temperature of warm or cool allows for harmony within the design. Basic warm colors are red, orange and yellow with cool colors being blue, green and purple.

The warm shades of pink, yellow and orange are feminine and energetic. The framed picture successfully uses papers with various intensities and equivalent temperatures.

The cool colors in this layout evoke a sense of peace and tranquility.

Monochromatic Color

By definition "mono" means "one" and "chrome" means "color"; therefore monochromatic is literally the use of one color. Within one color is a myriad shades and tints that when used create interest and definition in the design. Black and white can be added without ruining the effect because they are neutral colors. In many ways they strengthen the effect by defining borders or drawing attention to elements on the page.

The pictures in this layout are matted on red cardstock with the edges painted black to create a definition of borders so the pictures are not lost on the background. Various shades of red are created in the title by adding black paint with a stipple brush to the letters. The stippling effect was added while the red paint was still wet, allowing the colors to blend.

Color Value

The value of color is the relative lightness or darkness of the hue (color). High-value colors are tints, those with white added to the pure color. Low-value colors are shades where black has been added. Dramatic results can occur when light and dark values are placed next to each other. Likewise a subtle effect can be achieved when low values are blended.

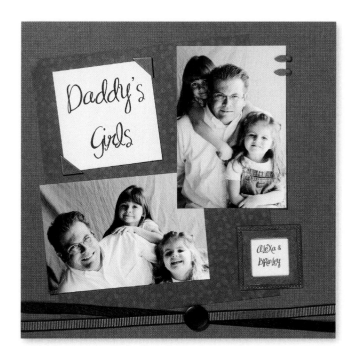

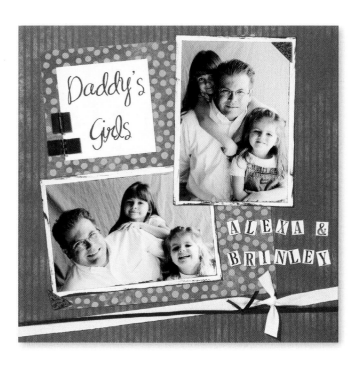

These two pages use the same pictures and basic design but have been created with different papers to show the varying values of blue. The low-value design (above) is more subdued and masculine in nature while the high-value layout is cheerful and lively.

Patterns

Patterns are the arrangement of shapes brought together to make predictable or random designs. They can establish the character and personality of a layout, helping to enhance the theme or mood of the photos.

Geometrics

Geometric designs are those that use shapes such as circles, squares, rectangles, triangles and/or diamonds to create the pattern. Geometric designs may be intimidating to work with due to their bold lines and usually intense, busy patterns. You can start out by using these prints in small amounts as accents on a page. As you become more willing to experiment, use the recommendations discussed in Scale (see page 11) to create balanced designs.

The patterns in this layout are expressly geometric using repetitive circle and square shapes. By masking some of the patterns with a strong title, ribbon and matted photos, the designs in the papers become secondary to the photos.

Florals

Floral patterns are typically inspired by colors and flowers found in nature and are most commonly reserved for feminine or heritage designs. Many companies have coordinating papers that take the guesswork out of choosing successful combinations. They come in a wide variety of colors and patterns to complement the mood for any design.

In this layout, a combination of scale is achieved through negative and positive floral images. The larger stencil-like flower uses a dark background to give weight. It is complemented by the medium-sized floral paper that features a light, airy design.

Scale

Scale, or the size of the print on your patterned paper, must be considered when combining papers in a layout. In terms of patterned paper, scale is the relationship between the size of the print on a paper compared to the size of the print on papers that are paired with it. Your selection of patterned papers can have a mix of large to small prints using plaids, stripes, florals, geometrics or random patterns when the scale is related correctly.

One recipe for success, when choosing three to four patterned papers to mix together on a layout, is to remember that the largest print should be 4 times the size of the second print with the third print or pattern being very small and repetitive. Your use of scale has a huge influence on the feeling of harmony in a layout.

Although this is a no-fail recipe for choosing the mix of sizes for your prints, there are other options. Create a focal point by exaggerating the size of a print, using a print that is 10 times the scale of the second print. You can repeat the same-scale prints, mixing small delicate prints or strong, large prints together. Don't be afraid to experiment with mixing unconventional combinations of prints, keeping in mind the relationship of scale.

Mixing and matching various scales

The biggest fear of working with patterned papers for many scrapbookers is mixing and matching various-sized scales of prints for aesthetically pleasing results. But with a little practice and a discerning eye, gorgeous results can be accomplished with ease.

The coordinating papers in this layout combine a mix of small-, medium- and large-scale prints for perfect balance. Note how the smallest scale polka-dot print is used as the largest piece of the layout. A busy script paper is accented to frame a large-scale floral print.

Mix small-, medium- and large-scale papers in a variety of patterns from different companies for great results. Here, the smallest scale floral print is used to cover the largest part of the layout and is layered over a medium-scale swirl paper. The top is covered with a strip of large-scale argyle patterned paper for visual balance.

Clockwise from the top: The prints in this color wheel range from small, polka-dot print to large-scale florals.

Placement

Apply the information you have learned thus far about color, value and scale when you select your papers. To determine the placement of your papers on a layout and to create balance on your page, you must consider the visual weight of the papers you've chosen. Patterned paper can visually be strongest because of a bold or heavy print. But a large-scale pattern does not always have more weight than a smaller print and a strong contrasting color can easily outweigh a bold print. To achieve balance by the use of color, pattern and placement, use different proportions of each paper so that they visually equal each other. For example, combine 70 percent of the paper that is visually the weakest with 25 percent of the second strongest and just 5 percent of your visually strongest paper.

You can create emphasis by changing the size, shape, position or color of your strongest element; use a color opposite or angle a patterned paper. Use any contrast carefully as it can become too forceful and alter the personality of the layout. If you are intimidated by the use of too many patterns, try some of these easier solutions for incorporating patterned paper successfully into stunning layouts: Use patterned papers as an accent or embellishment, use patterned papers in monochromatic colors or use a manufacturer's coordinating product. This book is filled with simple ideas for getting the most out of your patterned papers; try some of these great ideas today!

Balanced photo placement

To create harmony in your layout, consider your photographs and other decorative elements while arranging your papers on the layout. A busy photograph most likely will get lost on a busy patterned paper as will a dark photo on dark paper. Place your photo on the paper that will complement it best, or mat your photo on solid paper so it is not directly on patterned paper; it helps your photo become more the focal point when a solid paper gives your eye a place to rest in a mix of patterns.

Create focus for a black-and-white photograph by matting it against the visually strongest paper and placing it in the center of the page. Note how strips cut from a soft palette of different patterns, layered and stitched to the page background, create harmony. The bold, printed quote stands out against the pale background, contrasting with the soft stamped letters and numbers.

Balance is achieved in this layout through a pleasing mix of scale, color and placement. Using a mix of low-value colors and a wide strip of a small-scale patterned paper stitched to the page is a successful touch. The visually strongest papers are torn, layered and used as an accent. The photo easily becomes the focus when framed with a round shape and lighter color.

Storage & Organization

After you have all those wonderful patterned papers, how do you organize and store them so they are easy to see and quick to access? You can organize papers by separating them into colors like red, orange, yellow, green, blue, purple, brown, gray/black and white. Using this method makes it easier to combine patterned papers from different manufacturers that may coordinate well together and you can incorporate your solid papers in with the patterned papers.

There are many ways to store your papers; you must consider what is right for your scrapbooking needs and your space. Do you have a place dedicated to scrapbooking or do you need a mobile scrapbook station? Papers need to be stored in a cool and dry place with an ideal temperature of 75 degrees Fahrenheit or lower. Keep them away from high humidity and out of direct sunlight.

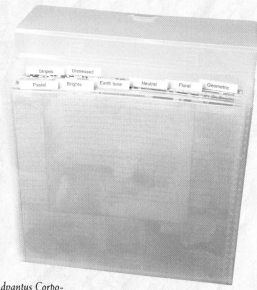

Cropper Hopper/Advantus Corporation's 12 x 12" Paper Organizers come in handy for smaller or portable patterned paper collections.

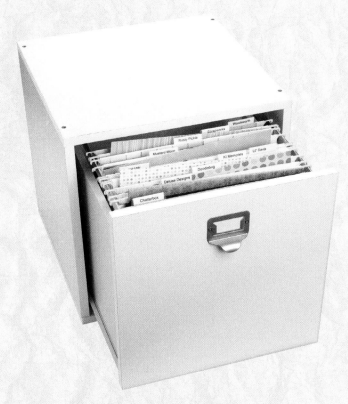

You can also sort patterned papers into color families (above), such as neutrals, pastels, brights and earth tones, or separate papers by manufacturers—many of which have custom-coordinating papers in colors that make it easy to use all papers in one line. Further, you can separate patterned papers by pattern, storing together all florals, geometrics, stripes, distressed, etc.

The best method of storing paper is flat, with no edges exposed that may get bent. If flat storage takes up too much room, there are products that have been developed for vertical storage with reinforcement for the papers so they won't droop or bend. If you have only a few papers, you can use a small organizer that can also double as a portable tote. An accordion file folder (above) is another storage solution for quick organization; it allows you to separate papers into many categories that are easy to view and access.

Crop In Style's Store In Style modular storage solutions, including this cube with a drawer, are easy to assemble and can accommodate any burgeoning paper collection.

Stackable paper trays are a good way to store papers flat, and you can add as many trays as needed. File folders are used in the same way, but the paper is stored vertically in plastic holders (right). There are many wire racks available. These are more permanent fixtures and come in many sizes, there are also racks with pullout trays. These racks make your papers easy to view. Plastic craft drawers will also hold a lot of papers and keep them protected from dust. The most permanent and lightfast storage method is the drawer and cabinet unit available made specifically for scrapbookers (above left). Using the organization and storage system that works best for you will help you become more efficient and effective in completing your scrapbook pages.

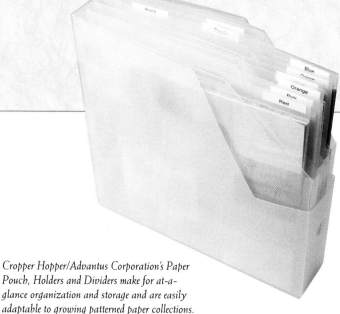

Cropper Hopper/Advantus Corporation's Paper Pouch, Holders and Dividers make for at-a-glance organization and storage and are easily adaptable to growing patterned paper collections.

Chapter ONE

Excitement, joy and hope come with the birth of a new baby—not to mention sleepless nights and endless diaper changes. Without question these experiences will be preserved as timeless treasures, forever contained in family albums. Choosing appropriate papers and techniques is essential in creating baby pages. In this chapter, you will learn how to effectively use patterns and colors to complement tender baby photographs, as well as create original patterns with the computer and alter papers with the ease of a pen.

Paige

COORDINATING

Create an eclectic look by combining several patterns and aging techniques. Layer checked border along the bottom of floral paper. Brush the edges of accent strips with brown chalk ink. Create a photo mat by tearing striped paper along one side and inking all edges with chalk ink. Crumple red paper and age with sandpaper, then layer with yellow polka-dot paper and machine stitch to striped paper. Adhere photo with dimensional adhesive. Tear floral paper diagonally at one corner; accent with eyelets and ribbon. Create journaling with rub-on letters and use letter stickers placed on ribbon and circle tiles to create the title.

Brandi Ginn

SUPPLIES: Patterned paper, rub-on letters, letter stickers, and tag (Chatterbox); circle tiles (Little Black Dress Designs); chalk ink (Tsukineko); adhesive (Therm O Web); ribbon

Floral Variation

Paint the edges of patterned paper using a sponge brush and acrylic paint. Use a foam stamp and paint to create a scroll border and paint metal accents.

SUPPLIES: Patterned paper, metal accents, and acrylic paint (Making Memories); Pink cardstock (Bazzill); brads (Happy Hammer); adhesive (Therm O Web)

Monochromatic Variation

Layer a striped border along lower edge of plum paper. For photo mats, layer various shades of plum paper and mat with photo corners. Create the title using metal letters and accent the layout with ribbon.

SUPPLIES: Plum patterned paper (Carolee's Creations); striped, floral patterned papers, and metal letters (Making Memories); crackle patterned paper (Keeping Memories Alive); photo corners (Canson); adhesive (Therm O Web); ribbon

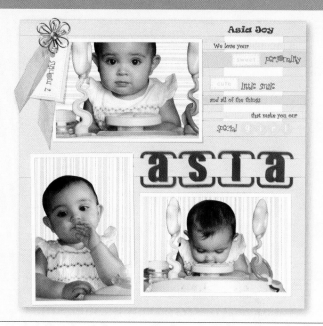

Asia Joy
ACCENT

Soften silhouette-cropped baby photos with a pastel-striped paper background. Print photos with white borders. Use a craft knife to crop backgrounds from photos leaving borders intact. Replace the background with striped paper. Print journaling on cardstock and cut into strips. Attach letter clips to cardstock strip for the title.

Pam Klassen
Photos: Janetta Abucejo Wieneke, Memory Makers Books

SUPPLIES: Striped paper, stickers (Paper Fever); lavender cardstock (Bazzill); letter clips (Scrapworks); flower brad (Karen Foster Design); adhesive (Therm O Web); craft knife

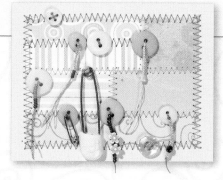

Baubled Patchwork
EMBELLISHMENT

Sew a variety of papers and baby items to theme a paper patchwork. Follow instructions below to create patchwork. Use embroidery floss to sew on diaper pin.

Pam Klassen

SUPPLIES: Striped and circle-patterned papers (Paper Fever); striped paper (SEI); swirl, floral paper (Treehouse Designs); brown paper (Design Originals); beads (JewelCraft); buttons (Junkitz); adhesive (Therm O Web); pins

Vintage Variation

Darker colors, vintage papers and a themed quote give this patchwork embellishment an old-fashioned look.

Pam Klassen

SUPPLIES: Patterned papers, quote (Diane's Daughters); buttons (Junkitz); beads (Jewel-Craft); adhesive (Therm O Web)

TIP: *Use this technique to replace a background that is too dark or cluttered, or create a theme: masculine, vintage or holiday.*

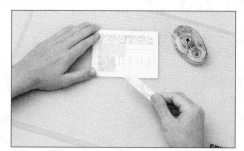

1 Cut papers to fit together in a rectangle and tack in place with adhesive.

2 Machine sew with zigzag stitch around outside of papers, then along all seams, changing thread colors. Pull ends to the back and tie.

3 Add buttons with needle and thread, pulling threads to the front, tie in front of button. Add beads using the needle, knot threads at the end of beads.

Daddy's Angel

BACKGROUND

Using monochromatic patterned paper as the background in soft colors adds a hint of texture and design. Brush acrylic paint on a foam stamp to create the scroll accents on the background paper and allow to dry. Tear pink striped and yellow patterned papers along one side and layer to create an oversized photo mat. Cover a large slide mount with pink paper and use a foam stamp and acrylic paint to add a scroll design. Create title with rub-on letters and accent with flower tile and tag. Accent layout with painted metal hinges, photo anchors and paper flowers attached with brads. Hand write journaling on a tag and accent with pink ribbon.

Brandi Ginn
Photo: Donald Bryant Sr., Aurora, Colorado

SUPPLIES: Pink patterned paper (KI Memories); yellow patterned paper (Anna Griffin); metal accents, rub-ons, paper flowers, brads, title stamp (Making Memories); corner scroll stamp (Hobby Lobby); large slide mount (Design Originals); acrylic paint (DecoArt); ribbon (Offray); adhesive (Therm O Web)

TIP: *Create a slightly variegated look to painted accents by loosely mixing dark and white paint. Apply with finger or sponge brush and allow to dry.*

A Boy With Silly Faces

MONOCHROMATIC

Inspired by the patterns and colors found within the baby's shirt, a bright monochromatic design was achieved. Cut checkered paper 8½ x 12", place on red dot paper and machine stitch together. Mat larger photos on white paper and adhere. Place smaller photos on random dot paper, accenting with painted metal hinges. Cut three tags from textured cardstock, crumple and paint the edges with acrylic paint. Create the title using alphabet stamps and acrylic paint. Finish title by using a small jewelry tag attached with a red brad. Print journaling on a transparency, adhere to red cardstock. Paint metal letter with white acrylic paint and layer on cardstock and a square tag.

Brandi Ginn
Photos: Rachel Scarborough, Thornton, Colorado

SUPPLIES: Checked and dotted paper (Pebbles); red cardstock (Bazzill); metal accents, rub-ons, square tag (Making Memories); transparency (Grafix); acrylic paint (Delta); alphabet stamps (Ma Vinci's Reliquary); jewelry tag (Avery); brad (Karen Foster Design); adhesive (Therm O Web)

Baby Aaron

CREATE YOUR OWN

Use a baby-boy clip art image to create patterned paper. Scan a baby portrait from clip art book. Work with the image in any image-editing software program to size the image and change its color. Follow the steps below to create the patterned paper. Insert text and print pages on cardstock. Print journaling on lighter cardstock, matching font color to page. Print small image for photo frame and embellish with ribbon.

Pam Klassen

Photos: Angela Siemens, Rosenort, Manitoba, Canada

SUPPLIES: Cardstock (Bazzill); baby-boy clip art (Dover Publications); photo corners (Canson); frame (Pebbles); adhesive (Therm O Web); ribbon

1 Scan clip art image from book. Use image-editing software to resize the image and repeat it to create a pattern on the page. Change the image color. For the first page, size images to fill spaces and add text.

2 Print pages on cardstock. Print small image on photo paper to mount in frame.

Garden Baby

INSPIRATION

Inspiration can be pulled from objects found within photos to enhance the overall design of the page. Cut patterned paper to 11 x 11" and place it slightly offset on red cardstock. Use a machine with a zigzag stitch to secure paper to the cardstock. Set photo askew from patterned paper and adhere with black photo corners. Create the title using a tag template, letter stickers and die-cut stickers rubbed with orange chalk. Finish the tag with ribbon and a button accent. Repeat the same tag design for journaling.

Brandi Ginn
Photo: Donald Bryant Sr., Aurora, Colorado

SUPPLIES: Patterned paper (Rusty Pickle); red and green cardstocks (Bazzill); letter stickers (Wordsworth); photo corners (Canson); letter die cuts (Foofala); chalk (Deluxe Designs); buttons (Junkitz); ribbon; adhesive (Therm O Web)

TIP: *Don't be afraid to place design elements within the empty spaces of photos. By doing so, continuity and flow is established.*

Bucket Head

COORDINATING

Coordinating papers allow the designer to effectively achieve balance in color and pattern. Cut striped paper 3 x 11" and place along the bottom. Ink and roll the edges of polka-dot and floral paper and layer on striped paper. Finish the border with a die-cut strip. Sew a zigzag stitch with a machine across the top and bottom edge. Repeat inking, tearing and layering techniques to create an additional photo mat. Conceal journaling on a tag placed within a stitched envelope. Use letter stickers to create the title and accent with buttons and ribbon.

Brandi Ginn

SUPPLIES: Patterned paper, letter stickers, sewn envelope, tags (Chatterbox); blue cardstock (Bazzill); chalk ink (Tsukineko); alphabet stamps (Hero Arts); ribbon; adhesive (Therm O Web)

TIP: *Print directly on die-cut tags in a color to match chalk ink by first printing on white paper. Then place the element on the paper over the printed text and run it through the printer again.*

Sweet Baby Boy

ALTER

Create plaid paper for a sweet, baby-boy page. Follow the steps below to alter the paper. Layer altered paper on cardstock; top the page with a strip of script paper. Separate papers with ribbon. Create title with sticker letters and conchos. Print journaling on cardstock and cut in strips, accent with ribbons and attach with brads. Mount photo over self-adhesive zipper.

Pam Klassen
Photo: Angela Siemens,
Rosenort, Manitoba, Canada

SUPPLIES: Striped paper (Paper Fever); script paper (7 Gypsies); cardstock (Bazzill); letter stickers (SEI); zipper (Junkitz); conchos, brads (Scrapworks); frame (Pebbles); adhesive (Therm O Web); ribbon; brads

TIP: *Use this technique to add stripes to any style paper, changing colors to coordinate with your layout.*

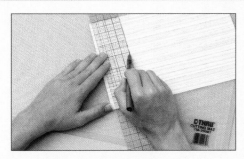

1 Draw lines across striped paper with a ruler and fine-tip marker. Vary pressure on pen tip and rock pen back and forth while drawing to create a rough look.

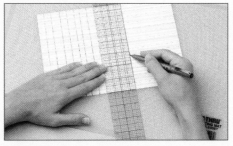

2 Space lines similar distances apart to preprinted lines: ¼", ⅜", and ½".

Chapter TWO

Birthdays are a time of celebration for young and old alike! After capturing those moments on film, preserve them in your albums with a combination of patterned papers that reflect the celebration. In the following pages, you will find inspiration to create patterned paper from die-cut shapes, tear monochromatic papers into a birthday cake, alter your pattern with beads and create a bright pocket for birthday memorabilia. Several additional ideas will inspire you to create personalized albums with fun patterned papers.

Birthday Girl

COORDINATING

Coordinate unrelated papers by combining related colors. Layer 5½" wide yellow plaid paper on the left side of the background paper. Tear the end off diamond paper, leaving a 7" wide strip, cut in half and adhere on top, placing in opposite corners. Secure ribbon to the back of page and tie in front. Add matted photo and letter stickers for title. Print journaling on transparency; adhere under edges of papers and behind frame.

Pam Klassen
Photos: Brandi Ginn

SUPPLIES: Pink script patterned paper (Rusty Pickle); yellow plaid paper (KI Memories); diamond paper (K & Company); pastel square paper (PSX Design); letter stickers (Wordsworth); paint (Delta); metal frame (Making Memories); ribbon

Pastel Variation

Beyond the relationship of colors shared by these papers, there is a circle pattern that is repeated in each print.

SUPPLIES: Background patterned paper (Autumn Leaves); green paper (KI Memories); pastel plaid paper (PSX Design); rainbow paper (Karen Foster Design); sticker letters (Wordsworth); paint (DecoArt); metal frame, ribbon charm (Making Memories); ribbon

Bright Variation

Create a bright birthday page by using an eclectic mix of bright stripes with a soft floral pastel print.

SUPPLIES: Bright striped patterned paper (NRN Designs); pink and yellow striped paper (Treehouse Designs); floral paper (Paper Adventures); cardstock (Bazzill); letter stickers (Wordsworth); paint (DecoArt); metal frame (Making Memories); ribbon

Brinley Turns 3

ACCENT

Creatively use patterned papers in place of the usual ribbons and fibers. Cut ½" strips of patterned paper and use to frame sequential pictures throughout the layout. Embellish square tags with rub-on numbers and add an eyelet. Use a ⅛" strip of patterned paper instead of fiber to finish the tag. Create the title on a premade tag using alphabet stamps and black ink. Use solvent ink to stamp the number 3 on a square tile and adhere with dimensional adhesive. Finish the tag with eyelets and embroidery floss.

Brandi Ginn

SUPPLIES: Striped patterned paper, premade tag (KI Memories); orange patterned paper (Scrapworks); blue, white and orange cardstocks (Bazzill); alphabet stamps (Wordsworth); number stamp (All Night Media); square tags, rub-on numbers, embroidery floss (Making Memories); square tiles (Little Black Dress Designs); brad (Lasting Impressions); solvent ink (Tsukineko); adhesive (Therm O Web)

2005 Birthday Cards

EMBELLISHMENT

Combine patterned papers and coordinating accents to create embellishments that can be used within a well-designed layout. Follow the steps below to cover an existing library card with various patterned papers and machine stitch each side closed. Place a strip of blue patterned paper at a diagonal across the front; wrap around and secure in back. Use die-cut letters, numbers and a label maker for the title. Accent the embellishment with brads, star button and page pebble.

Brandi Ginn

SUPPLIES: Patterned paper (KI Memories); orange cardstock (Bazzill); library card (Rusty Pickle); die-cut letters (QuicKutz); label maker (Dymo); brads (Lasting Impressions); star button (Doodlebug Design); page pebble (Creative Imaginations); Memory Tape Runner adhesive (Therm O Web)

1 Trace a library pocket on the back of patterned paper and cut out.

2 Cover the pocket with the patterned paper on the front and back, securing with adhesive.

Birthday Cake

BACKGROUND

Coordinate background paper and page elements with paint. Maggie created a layout to capture Tyler's enjoyment of his birthday cake. Coordinate Making Memories background patterned paper with other elements of the page by painting the edges of papers, photos and title with matching paint. Machine-stitch layers of tulle across bottom of page and embellish with painted metal accents and tags. Print the journaling on a transparency and attach to background with staples.

Maggie Holmes for Making Memories

SUPPLIES: Background patterned paper, tag, alphabet, paint, ribbon, hinges, brads, photo corners, staples (Making Memories); tags (American Tag); ink (Ranger); ribbon (Stampin' Up!); tulle

Sasha 12

MONOCHROMATIC

Tear and stitch a monochromatic paper birthday cake to frame a photo. Machine stitch light blue paper onto background paper. Tear paper pieces to create a cake; stitch pieces to light paper. Cover stencil letters with patterned paper and cut out centers with craft knife. Back letters with light paper and stitch edges to page. Add words inside letters. Mount title letters on a variety of patterned papers and attach to mat with brads, stitch to page. Frame preprinted word in concho; add photos.

Pam Klassen
Photos: Michele Gerbrandt, Memory Makers

SUPPLIES: Plaid background, striped, polka-dot patterned papers (Printworks); wavy paper (Provo Craft); star paper (Hot Off The Press); sticker letters, metal embellishments (Scrapworks); adhesive (Therm O Web)

Happy Birthday

CREATE YOUR OWN

Inspired by shapes and patterns found within the party décor, Brandi created her own patterned paper. Follow the steps below to create the background for the design. Mat photos on green patterned paper and adhere. Fill in empty spaces with captions made from patterned paper and die-cut letters. Print journaling on white cardstock, cut into a tag shape and rub the edges with chalk. Finish the tag with ribbon and a button. To create the accordion embellishment, cut two pieces of patterned paper 4½ x 12". Score at 4½" intervals, alternating score lines on the front and back; fold back and forth. There will be paper left over; use this to adhere the second accordion-folded section. Secure accordion book with ribbon and zipper pull.

Brandi Ginn

SUPPLIES: Die-cut and punched patterned papers, green patterned paper (Lasting Impressions); pink patterned paper (Doodlebug Design); red cardstock (Bazzill); die-cut letters and shapes (QuicKutz); chalk (Deluxe Designs); button (Making Memories); zipper pull (Junkitz); ribbon (Offray); Zots adhesive (Therm O Web)

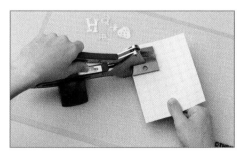

1 Use a QuickKutz tool to punch die-cut shapes from patterned paper.

2 Place and adhere shapes randomly across page allowing room for pictures and title.

3 Fill in empty spaces with captions and, if needed, more punched shapes.

It's a Party!

DOUBLE-SIDED

Cut and fold double-sided papers to hold extra birthday photos. Cut three pieces of double-sided paper 4" wide. Center tag one inch up on bottom of solid paper strip and trace top 1¼" of tag. Cut shape with craft knife, cut out an additional ½" rectangle above top of tag. Fold paper at the base of cut tag. Adhere short folded section to page background so the front reaches bottom of page. Stamp "fun" on tags in monochromatic colors. Adhere squares to tops of tags and punch a hole, add small tags with jump rings. Attach vellum headings with brads. Use letter stickers for title and attach to top of page with eyelets. Add journaling and additional photos under flaps. Add clay phrase embellishment.

Pam Klassen

Photos: Tammy Stegall, Reedley, California

SUPPLIES: All patterned papers (American Crafts); letter stickers (Wordsworth); alphabet stamps (Making Memories); jump rings (Junkitz); clay phrase (Li'l Davis Designs); adhesive (Therm O Web); eyelets and brads, ¼" hole punch, craft knife

Jessica

COORDINATING

Coordinate soft patterned papers for a girl's birthday layout. Join two half-sheets of coordinating paper with a border sticker down the center of the page. Layer short torn strips on either side of center. Cut a small rectangle in transparency paper to create a template to trace boxes above and below letter stickers. Cut title and number from computer font. Tie tag and embellishment to number with fiber. Print journaling on vellum and use foam adhesive to adhere flower stickers.

Pam Klassen

Photos: Brenda Muzzy, Dinuba, California

SUPPLIES: All patterned papers, flower stickers, small letter stickers (Paper Fever); zipper pull (Junkitz); adhesive (Therm O Web)

Birthday Boy

ALTER

Alter patterned paper using dimensional adhesives and tiny glass marbles. Cut striped patterned paper 2½ x 8½" and place within the bottom third of the page. Cut 3½" squares of patterned paper and place randomly along the right side of the page. Adhere pictures in a straight line over the patterned squares. Follow the steps below to alter a large piece of patterned paper using dimensional adhesive and mixed tiny glass marbles. Mat photo on cardstock and secure with foam adhesive. Use letter stickers to create the title. Print journaling on a transparency and adhere with a spray adhesive to a premade tag.

Brandi Ginn
Photos: Rachel Scarborough, Thornton, Colorado

SUPPLIES: Patterned paper, light green cardstock, premade tag (KI Memories); letter stickers (Deluxe Designs); Zips adhesive (Therm O Web); blue and silver tiny glass marbles; transparency (Grafix)

Birthday Boy

At first Dylan wasn't too sure what to do with his cupcake. First, he tried to touch the flame of the candle—yikes! Then Daddy had to help him stick just one finger in the frosting and lick it. After that he caught on REAL quick and made a huge mess!
August 8, 2004 --one year old!

TIP: *Avoid touching the adhesive with your fingers; the oils from your skin will compromise the adhesion. Work in small increments adding glass beads as you go.*

1 Cut patterned paper 7 x 7¾".

2 Following the design found within the patterned paper, slowly adhere Zips adhesive.

3 Mix silver and blue glass marbles together and press into adhesive; shake off excess.

Chapter THREE

It was once said that parents are people who spend one-half of their time worrying how a child will turn out, and the rest of the time wondering when a child will turn in. As precious little blessings, children can make us laugh and try our patience. Their relationships with others and the characters we see developing are tender, fragile and ever-changing. Contained within this chapter are ideas for neutral and monochromatic designs, punched patterns and sewn ribbon to inspire original creations reflective of the blissful child.

True Siblings

BACKGROUND

Warm photos with dark backgrounds with carefully selected colors and patterns. Cut striped patterned paper 6½" wide and place on red cardstock. Layer with checked paper and machine-stitch zigzag pattern along the top and bottom. Adhere the photos at slight angles. Double mat the top photo on script and gray patterned paper. Create a multimedia title using stencils, tiles with letter pebbles placed on top, tile letters, metal letters, stickers and label maker.

Brandi Ginn

SUPPLIES: Striped paper (Chatterbox); checked gray paper (Mustard Moon); script paper (Carolee's Creations); red cardstock (Bazzill); stencil letters (7 Gypsies); gray tiles (Little Black Dress Designs); pebble letters, letter sticker (Creative Imaginations); tile letters (Doodlebug Design); metal letters (Making Memories); letter sticker (Wordsworth); label maker (Dymo); adhesive (Therm O Web)

Cool Variation

Create the title by painting the cardstock with white acrylic paint. After the paint has dried, use rub-on letters to create the title.

SUPPLIES: Striped patterned paper (Deluxe Designs); blue and purple patterned paper (Wordsworth); light blue patterned paper (Mustard Moon); paisley patterned paper (Chatterbox); acrylic paint (Plaid); rub-on letters, metal accent (Making Memories); adhesive (Therm O Web)

Earthtone Variation

Embellish a rectangle tag by embossing the edges with gold powder and accent with a gold clock face and spiral clip. Use letter stickers on the tag to create the title. For the gold writing, stamp letters with a watermark inkpad and heat set with gold embossing powder.

SUPPLIES: Cork patterned paper (Rusty Pickle); green patterned paper, letter stickers and alphabet stamps (Wordsworth); brown patterned paper (Design Originals); olive patterned paper (Mustard Moon); green cardstock (Bazzill); tag (Making Memories); clock (7 Gypsies); circle clip; watermark ink (Tsukineko); embossing powder (PSX Design); adhesive (Therm O Web)

We Are Blessed

ACCENT

Accent a page with floral borders and a collaged journaling tag. Border top and bottom of green background with pink cardstock and layer two strips of patterned paper along seams. Cut circular photo with a circle cutter, then cut slightly larger circle in cardstock and cut a square around the centered circle to complete the frame. Collage frame with torn papers and mount on stamped tag with transparencies. Adhere journaled tag to green background and tie tags together with a ribbon. Add jounaling to the photo using any image-editing software. Reprint smaller photo on transparency.

Pam Klassen

SUPPLIES: Diamond patterned paper (SEI); floral heritage paper (Anna Griffin); peach, green cardstocks (Bazzill); pink floral paper (Chatterbox); text stamp (Inkadinkado) transparencies (Artchix Studio); adhesive (Therm O Web); 5/16" hole punch; ribbon

Masculine Variation

Alter a fun book to preserve a moment of history. Use a heritage photo with jute and masculine colors.

Pam Klassen

SUPPLIES: Western patterned papers (K & Company); cardstock (Bazzill); nailhead (JewelCraft); composition book (AMPAD); adhesive (Therm O Web); hole punch; twine; ribbon

Fairydust Princess

EMBELLISHMENT

Alter a mini composition book to hold sentimental treasures. Following the steps below, cut patterned paper to fit inside front and back covers. Cover label of book with patterned paper and decorate with stickers, jewel, glitter and crafts items. Cut photo to fit in concho and secure on cover. Add bead to ribbon and tie in front. Adhere photo and letter stickers to the inside of the book.

Pam Klassen
Photo: Ryan Watamura, Reedley, California

SUPPLIES: Dark pink script paper (Karen Foster Design); light pink, green circle paper (Paper Fever); composition book (AMPAD); letter stickers (Paper Fever, Wordsworth); rhinestone (JewelCraft); glitter (DecoArt) concho (Scrapworks); Zots adhesive (Therm O Web); bead; ribbon

1 Gently pull out pages from the spine of the notebook.

2 Glue ribbon to the inside of front cover, near spine. Adhere papers inside notebook covers, covering ribbon and meeting in the center of the spine.

3 Cut paper to cover front label, collage with papers, stickers, memorabilia and photo. Add bead to the ribbon and tie in front.

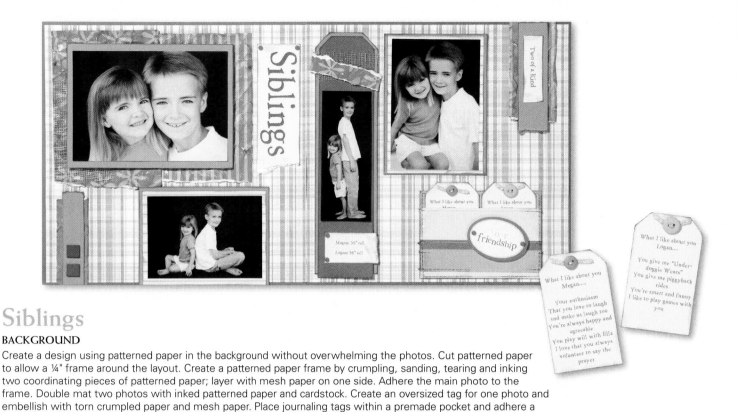

Siblings

BACKGROUND

Create a design using patterned paper in the background without overwhelming the photos. Cut patterned paper to allow a ¼" frame around the layout. Create a patterned paper frame by crumpling, sanding, tearing and inking two coordinating pieces of patterned paper; layer with mesh paper on one side. Adhere the main photo to the frame. Double mat two photos with inked patterned paper and cardstock. Create an oversized tag for one photo and embellish with torn crumpled paper and mesh paper. Place journaling tags within a premade pocket and adhere a preprinted oval title with foam adhesive to the pocket. Embellish paper accents with buttons and tiles.

Brandi Ginn

SUPPLIES: Patterned paper, premade pocket, preprinted oval title (Chatterbox); mesh paper (Magenta); rust and olive cardstocks (Bazzill); tiles (Little Black Dress Designs); buttons (Junkitz); chalk ink (Tsukineko); ribbon (Making Memories); adhesive (Therm O Web)

TIP: *Have your photo developer print photos in wallet and 3½ x 5" sizes allowing you to be able to include a smaller version of the entire photo on your layout.*

The Eyes Have It

MONOCHROMATIC

Start by creating the background using foam stamps and acrylic paint (see page 47 for step-by-step directions). Cut striped paper 4" wide and adhere, placing ribbon over the seam. Mat all photos on a lighter shade of brown cardstock and place throughout the layout. To create the ribbon accent, set two eyelets for each ribbon directly across from each other. Weave ribbon through eyelets and tie a knot on top. Accent with patterned paper placed diagonally in the corners and create the title using alphabet stamps and chalk ink.

Brandi Ginn

SUPPLIES: Patterned paper (Chatterbox); brown cardstock (Bazzill); foam stamp (Making Memories); acrylic paint (Plaid); large alphabet stamps (Ma Vinci's Reliquary); small alphabet stamps (Hero Arts); chalk ink (Clearsnap); ribbon; adhesive (Therm O Web)

TIP: *This is a fun idea that can be used for any page theme by simply changing the theme of papers used.*

Celebrate Friendship

CREATE YOUR OWN

Create the excitement of child's play with bright layers of punched, patterned papers against a dark background. Print journaling before punching out squares. Then follow the steps below to create colorful background. Add letter stickers and transparency sentiments.

Pam Klassen
Photo: Chelle Sigumoto, Reedley, California

SUPPLIES: Blue patterned paper (Scrapworks); green papers (Printworks, Scrapbook Wizard, Treehouse Designs); multicolored papers (Magenta); orange paper (Karen Foster Design); pink papers (Carolee's Creations, Karen Foster Design, Paper Adventures, Wordsworth); yellow paper (Printworks); letter stickers (Wordswoth); transparency film (Carolee's Creations); adhesive (Therm O Web)

1 Punch squares from a variety of patterned papers in four different sizes.

2 Layer two smaller size squares off center on largest squares.

3 Adhere layered squares ¼" apart on card-stock background.

Brinley

INSPIRATION

Choose papers inspired by patterns found in the clothing of the photo's subject. Create the oversized border by layering various patterned papers and accent with buttons and photo anchors. Cut yellow flowers from patterned paper, chalk the edges and cover with an oversized page pebble. Double mat the photo on cardstock and patterned paper, then accent with painted photo corners. Cover a coin holder with patterned paper and use to frame a dot word. Print the title on a transparency and paint the back. Adhere to pink paper stamped with scroll image and finish with a stencil covered in patterned paper. Embellish with ribbon and painted metal accents.

Brandi Ginn

SUPPLIES: Striped patterned paper, shaped buttons (Doodlebug Design); dark pink, flower, orange patterned papers (KI Memories); pink mosaic paper (Paper Fever); pink, green patterned papers (Scrapworks); peach cardstock (Bazzill); page pebbles, dot word (Creative Imaginations); photo anchors, metal accents (Making Memories); coin holder (Hobby Lobby); stencil (7 Gypsies); transparency; acrylic paint (Plaid); scroll stamp (Hero Arts); chalk ink (Tsukineko); ribbon; adhesive (Therm O Web)

Sweet

COORDINATING

Use coordinating papers to create a balanced design. On the first page, cut triangles from coordinating patterned paper and place at angles in each corner. For the ribbon accent, set four eyelets along patterned paper and cardstock parallel to each other. Weave ribbon as though lacing a shoe and tie a bow. Mat photos on cardstock and patterned paper. Conceal journaling behind a folded piece of patterned paper embellished with foam stamps and acrylic paint; secure with photo anchors. Create the title by painting metal letters in various shades of pink and attach to polka-dot ribbon with jump rings and ribbon. For the second page, frame pictures in oversized slide mounts covered with patterned paper and tie together with ribbon (see page 63 for step-by-step instructions). Cover pieces of chipboard with patterned paper and create an accordion-folded book by fan-folding pink cardstock. Embellish the inside with pictures, ribbon, acrylic paint and foam stamps.

Brandi Ginn

SUPPLIES: Patterned paper, metal plaque, metal letters, photo anchors, foam stamps, cream paint, pink ribbon (Making Memories); pink, brown cardstocks (Bazzill); deep coral acrylic paint (Delta); baby-pink Papier paint (Plaid); dark pink and polka-dot ribbons; alphabet stamps (Hero Arts); chalk ink (Clearsnap); adhesive (Therm O Web)

Sisters, Best Friends

ALTER

Sew a sweet flower-filled ribbon between layers of torn paper. Tear vertical strips of patterned paper and follow the steps below to alter the script paper, inserting fabric leaves randomly in stitched seams. Trim stitched paper to 11" square and adhere to cardstock. Offset photos on cardstock mats, print quote on vellum and mount with brads. Accent the first letters of the title by printing on cardstock and placing on tags.

Pam Klassen

Photos: Ryan Watamura, Reedley, California

SUPPLIES: Background paper (Chatterbox); script patterned paper (Karen Foster Design); peach cardstock (Bazzill); fabric leaves (Artchix Studio); ribbon (Michaels); metal-rimmed tags (Avery); adhesive (Therm O Web); brads

1 Tear the script paper vertically in strips.

2 Mount torn edge of paper onto ribbon with adhesive and insert stems of fabric leaves. Machine stitch close to paper along ribbon.

Chapter FOUR

Feminine as it relates to design is often thought of as only flowery or fancy. But colors and patterns combined with floral detail can offer a more complete package. While checkerboard or striped patterns used with solid cardstock may reflect a masculine tone, those same patterns coupled with floral or baroque patterns convey femininity. The same holds true for colors: A pink and purple plaid would be an appropriate color choice for a girl page while the same pattern in blue and green would be better suited for a boy. Let's explore more fun uses of patterned papers for feminine appeal.

Sisters Friends

BACKGROUND

Layer patterns and colors to create eclectic pieces of art. Cut strips of patterned paper in various widths and lengths; ink the edges of several papers and layer on red patterned paper. Cut a piece of fabric paper 1¼ x 12", ink the edges and adhere to the top of the page with a zigzag stitch on the top and bottom. Stitch floral paper to the background and place matted photo on top. Ink the edges of die-cut letters to create the title. Accent the layout with jute fiber and a vintage tag.

Brandi Ginn

SUPPLIES: Patterned paper, fabric paper, vintage tag, jute fiber (Me & My Big Ideas); letters (Foofala); chalk ink (Tsukineko); adhesive (Therm O Web)

Color Variation

To create the crisscross border, cut strips of patterned paper ¼" wide. Cross two strips in front, wrap around purple paper and secure in back.

SUPPLIES: Large and small floral paper, striped paper, photo anchors, rub-on letters (Making Memories); polka-dot paper, purple weave paper, rivets, flower snaps (Chatterbox); script paper (7 Gypsies); purple square paper, green patterned paper (Mustard Moon); purple cardstock (Bazzill); jump ring (Junkitz); ribbon (Offray); brads (Lasting Impressions); chalk (Deluxe Designs); adhesive (Therm O Web)

Pastel Variation

Freehand cut a flower from pink mosaic paper, chalk the edges and embellish with a flower-shaped button. Use letter stickers to create the title and accent the design with square tags decorated with flower-shaped buttons.

SUPPLIES: Blue striped paper, blue floral paper, shaped buttons (Doodlebug Design); blue patterned paper, pink floral paper, blue cardstock (KI Memories); pink mosaic paper (Paper Fever); pink patterned paper (Creative Imaginations); pink cardstock (Bazzill); chalk (Deluxe Designs); letter stickers (Wordsworth); square tags (Making Memories); adhesive (Therm O Web)

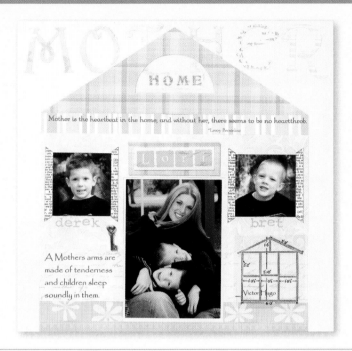

Mother

ACCENT

Paper piece a home of mother's love with pastel papers and quotes. Print a quote lengthwise across paper and cut into a strip for the top of the house. Cut various papers for the remaining pieces of the house, adding additional quotes. Mount photos behind window and door openings. Stamp names under windows and on mounted paper above door. Print title, and cut letters from a variety of papers. Adhere letter stickers under vellum on roof. Add transparency and key embellishments.

Pam Klassen
Photos: Ryan Watamura, Reedley, California

SUPPLIES: Floral, plaid, striped pattern papers (Chatterbox); lace paper (Autumn Leaves); script paper (7 Gyspies, Carolee's Creations, Design Originals); yellow cardstock (Bazzill); border accent (Diane's Daughters); vellum (Papers by Catherine); letter stamps (Hero Arts, PSX Design); letter stickers (Li'l Davis Designs); transparency, metal key (Artchix Studio); adhesive (Therm O Web)

TIP: *Use unconventional papers to piece shapes that match a theme; script paper for a cruise ship, floral paper for a family pet.*

Girlfriend

EMBELLISHMENT

Create a soft feminine title cut from template letters. Use a template to cut letters from papers of similar values. Follow steps below to create the title, cutting a ¼" wide frame to fit around the title.

Pam Klassen

SUPPLIES: Background patterned paper (KI Memories); pink papers (Carolees's Creations, Chatterbox, Hot Off The Press, Karen Foster Design); gold, green papers (Anna Griffin, Diane's Daughters); cardstock (Bazzill); letter template (EK Success); rhinestones (Jewel-Craft); foam spacers (Therm O Web); Gem-Tac liquid adhesive (Beacon Adhesives)

Color-Value Variation

Vary this look by simply changing the tone of the patterned papers as well as the letter template or font used to create the title.

SUPPLIES: Green, red patterned papers (Anna Griffin); purple patterned papers (Colorbök, Design Originals, Mustard Moon); cardstock (Bazzill); letter template (EK Success); rhinestones (JewelCraft); foam adhesive (Therm O Web); Gem-Tac glue (Beacon Adhesives)

1 Use a template to draw letters backward on the back of paper and cut out.

2 Mat various letters on rectangles adhered to 2½ x 12" background.

3 Adhere frame to background with foam spacers; glue rhinestone accents on letters.

Megan

BACKGROUND

Two patterned papers stitched together produces an original background. Cut orange patterned paper to 10½" square; mount on upper left-hand corner of pink checkerboard paper. Machine stitch zigzag pattern around the orange paper. Mat photos on pink and orange patterned paper; adhere. For ribbon accent along one photo mat, set two eyelets for each ribbon. String ribbons through and tie a knot on top. Mat this photo on foam core before adhering to the background. Frame smaller photo with a painted metal frame and attach with Super Tape. Apply rub-on letters to pink and orange ribbon; secure to background with page pebbles and conchos. Accent with a word dot tied with pink ribbon. Print journaling on transparency and lightly brush the back with acrylic paint; adhere with spray adhesive.

Brandi Ginn

SUPPLIES: Orange patterned paper (Karen Foster Design); checkerboard paper (Lasting Impressions); orange and pink paper (Wordsworth); ribbon; metal frame, rub-on letters, page pebbles, paint (Making Memories); word dot, spray adhesive (Creative Imaginations); conchos (Scrapworks); transparency; Super Tape adhesive (Therm O Web)

TIP: *Paint the entire metal checkerboard frame pink and let it dry. Using a small paintbrush, apply orange paint to every other square creating the checkerboard look.*

Brinley

MONOCHROMATIC

Soft monochromatic tones in feminine colors and patterns complement the delicate photos. Tear one side of patterned paper and stitch to pink cardstock along torn edge. Mat photos on a lighter shade of pink paper and place throughout the layout. Frame smaller photos with painted and chalked metal frames. Create the envelope and pocket embellishments using a template and decorate with rub-on letters and ribbon. Paint the rim of a circle tag with acrylic paint and use alphabet stamps and white embossing powder to print words on circle accent. Use painted letters for the title and accent the layout with rickrack and square snaps.

Brandi Ginn

SUPPLIES: Patterned paper, square snaps (Chatterbox); metal letters, frames, circle tag, rub-on letters, ribbon (Making Memories); chalk, envelope, pocket templates (Deluxe Designs); alphabet stamps (Hero Arts); embossing powder (PSX Design); Zots adhesive (Therm O Web)

TIP: *To successfully paint the metal letters, first adhere them to a paper plate using Zots adhesive. Using a matte finish acrylic paint and a sponge brush, carefully sweep a small amount of paint across the top. To avoid paint seeping into the letters, do not apply a lot of pressure. Apply two coats of paint, let dry and rub the edges with chalk.*

True Beauty

CREATE YOUR OWN

Design a precut window page with stamps, ink and accent with 3-D paint. Follow the steps below to create inked and painted background. Stamp letters on journaling block with paint, rub with ink, let dry. Add letter stickers and outline with 3-D paint. Tie tassels through metal embellishment. Add letter stickers under window openings.

Pam Klassen

Photos: Ryan Watamura, Reedley, California

SUPPLIES: Window Pages (C-Thru Ruler); pear stamp (A Stamp in the Hand); text stamp (Hero Arts); alphabet stamps (Ma Vinci's Reliquary); paint (Plaid); 3-D paint (DecoArt); carmel ink (Ranger); letter stickers (Colorbök, SEI); tassel (Provo Craft); adhesive (Therm O Web); metal leaf

1 Stamp pear shapes with paint across the page and let dry.

2 Water down ink and splatter across page. Stamp text across page. Use sponge applicator to rub ink around stamped pears.

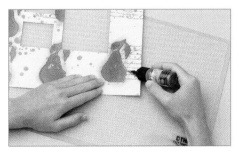

3 Draw an outline around each pear shape using 3-D paint with a fine-tip applicator.

Me

FABRIC

Fabrics can provide a unique texture and pattern for scrapbook pages. Sew fabric to red cardstock using a machine with a zigzag stitch and black thread. Create borders along the top and bottom using black trim. To create the photo mat, paint the edges of black cardstock with white acrylic paint and embellish one side with eyelets and various ribbons. Mat the photo on foam core and adhere to the fabric. Print bullet style journaling on red cardstock and accent with black buttons and brads. Use letter tiles for the title and initials.

Brandi Ginn

SUPPLIES: Fabric (Wamsutta); red, black cardstocks (Bazzill); black trim, dashed ribbon (Me & My Big Ideas); various ribbons; acrylic paint (Delta); flower eyelets (Creative Imaginations); black buttons, brads (Lasting Impressions); letter tiles (Deluxe Designs); metal flower, number rub-ons (Making Memories); Super Tape adhesive (Therm O Web)

TIP: *Secure fabric with Super Tape before stitching in place and use Super Tape to adhere journaling.*

Delight

COORDINATING

Warm-colored papers complement the sun's glow in the photos. Cut yellow polka-dot paper 5 x 11" and adhere to yellow cardstock. Layer with pink and orange patterned paper. Mat photos on pink cardstock and accent one photo with a strip of plaid paper, circle tacks and a metal washer. Re-create a stencil from pink cardstock by tracing a stencil and cutting out the letter with a craft knife. Place a large piece of plaid paper behind the stencil. Ink the edges of a dictionary definition sticker and adhere to the layout.

Brandi Ginn

SUPPLIES: Polka-dot patterned paper, circle tacks (Chatterbox); pink and orange patterned paper, plaid paper (Deluxe Designs); metal washer, dictionary definition sticker (Making Memories); chalk ink (Tsukineko); ribbon (Offray); foam adhesive, Memory Tape Runner adhesive (Therm O Web)

TIP: *Use a sharp craft knife to easily cut round edges in the stencil.*

God Gave Us Girls

ALTER

Cut away patterned paper background to create a new design. Follow the steps below to cut patterned paper and sandwich photos between papers. Print journaling and cut to fit metal-rimmed tags; attach to page with ribbons. Stamp names on tags and sew to page. Mat title border on striped paper and add letter stickers.

Pam Klassen
Photos: Ryan Watamura, Reedley, California

SUPPLIES: Floral, striped patterned papers (K & Company); green paper (Chatterbox); tags (Avery, handmade); love sticker (Pebbles); letter stickers (Wordsworth); ribbon; Memory Tape Runner adhesive (Therm O Web)

TIP: *Try cutting the background from patterned paper that has a graphic print, heritage print or sections of a bold plaid for layering over photos to create an interesting framing effect.*

1 Use a craft knife to cut out background around flowers and leaves, leaving outer edges of paper intact.

2 Trim selected photographs to fit behind cut out openings.

3 Adhere cut floral paper over striped background, sandwiching photos between the paper layers.

Chapter FIVE

Certain photos just call for the energy created by a graphic patterned paper. Use the following ideas as inspiration to incorporate graphic patterned papers in your layouts. Use graphic paper as a focal point, alter paper with spray paint, create a CD embellishment or cut a graphic title out of double-sided paper. All the ideas in this chapter will help you feel more comfortable using those big bold prints in your layouts.

Saving Summer

GRAPHIC

Create oversized letter for the focus and energy of this graphic page. Print the title repeatedly across paper, print and cut out letter. Cut two background papers so they join beneath the letter. Add photos, cutting the black-and-white photo to fit within the shape of the S. Cut journaling block to frame the focal photo and adhere the cross, printed on vellum, in the bottom corner. Attach letter with large rivets.

Pam Klassen

Photos: Angela Siemens, Rosenort, Manitoba, Canada

SUPPLIES: Swirl patterned paper (Reminiscence Papers); alphabet patterned paper (Rusty Pickle); vellum (SEI); metal rivets (Chatterbox); adhesive (Therm O Web)

Multicolor Variation

Try pulling colors from the photo backgrounds when selecting patterned papers for a custom-coordinated look.

SUPPLIES: Blue zebra patterned paper (Wordsworth); circle patterned paper (Carolee's Creations); vellum (Printworks); metal rivets (Chatterbox); adhesive (Therm O Web)

Monochromatic Variation

Using more monochromatic graphic papers helps photos stand out instead of competing with the background.

SUPPLIES: Retro, circle patterned papers (Sassafras Lass); vellum (Treehouse Designs); metal rivets (Chatterbox); adhesive (Therm O Web)

A Boy Is a Noise...

ACCENT

Accent with small amounts of patterned paper. Cut patterned paper and cardstock in various lengths and widths and adhere to green cardstock. Mat one photo on green cardstock adding a word tile embellished with blue ribbon. Create a multimedia quote using letter tiles, letter stickers, pebble letters and word beads.

Brandi Ginn
Photos: David Mayes, Lafayette, Colorado

SUPPLIES: Patterned paper, cardstock, letter tiles (Doodlebug Design); word tile (Junkitz); ribbon (Offray); letter stickers (Wordsworth); pebble letters (Li'l Davis Designs); word bead (Magnetic Poetry); adhesive (Therm O Web)

My Daughter

EMBELLISHMENT

Create graphic embellishments by altering CDs. Cut a circle of teal patterned paper and mount on a CD. Cover a mini DVD with letter paper and embellish with tile letters and label tape. Place the mini DVD off-center on the teal CD and accent with ribbon and a small picture.

Brandi Ginn

SUPPLIES: Teal patterned paper (KI Memories); letter paper (Deluxe Designs); letter tiles (Doodlebug Design); label tape (Dymo); ribbon (Me & My Big Ideas); adhesive (Therm O Web)

Bold Variaton

Embellish the CD with twill tape, circle clip, metal tag and a metal bottle cap. Decorate the mini DVD with a red slide mount and woven word. Adhere the mini DVD to the CD with foam adhesive.

SUPPLIES: Patterned paper (KI Memories); twill tape (Creek Bank Creations); spiral clip (Making Memories); metal tag (Creative Impressions); bottle cap (Li'l Davis Designs); slide mount (Scrapworks); woven word (Me & My Big Ideas); foam adhesive (Therm O Web)

Pastel Variation

Layer discs with patterned paper and premade embellishments. Apply liquid dimensional adhesive to a premade slide mount and let it dry. Punch a flower shape from patterned paper and accent with a button.

SUPPLIES: Patterned paper, premade accents (KI Memories); flower punch (EK Success); button (Junkitz); dimensional liquid adhesive (JudiKins); foam adhesive (Therm O Web)

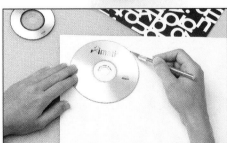

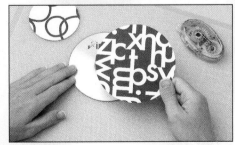

1 Use a craft knife or trace with a pencil around the CD and cut with scissors.

2 Apply adhesive to the back of cut paper and layer centered onto CD.

Kids came from all over the world to participate in this years

Summer Enrichment Program

Held at the University of Northern Colorado In Greeley   2004

Band

Dance Class

Summer Enrichment Program

BACKGROUND

Bringing focus to the graphic paper helps convey the energy of a young dance class. Layer strips of coordinating paper to the bottom and side of the background paper, covering seams with border stickers. Add matted photo, sticker title and journaling. Embellish with decorative eyelets.

Pam Klassen
Photo: Michele Gerbrandt, Memory Makers

SUPPLIES: Background patterned paper and border stickers (Sassafras Lass); small square paper (Paper Fever); letter stickers (Wordsworth); eyelets (Making Memories); adhesive (Therm O Web)

The Playground

MONOCHROMATIC

Cut and adhere monochromatic papers in graphic angles. Cut papers on angles and adhere next to each other across page background. Crop photos to fit down right side of page. Adhere large photo to page. Put clear sticker letters on patterned paper background and cut out. Adhere words to surround photo and add journaling tag to the arrow.

Pam Klassen
Photos: MaryAnn Klassen, Reedley, California

SUPPLIES: Striped, circle patterned paper (Creative Imaginations); small square paper (Heidi Grace Designs); large square patterned paper, floral paper (Two Busy Moms); blue squiggle paper (Scrapworks); letter stickers (Wordsworth); adhesive (Therm O Web)

conquered

They came They

THE PLAYGROUND

Grace & Casey

Brinley's Favorites

Color: Purple and pink

Food: Tuna fish

TV Show: Arthur, Big Clifford

Snack: Fishy Crackers

Least Favorite: Not pinch people

Thing to Do: Play with Strawberry Shortcake, and My Little Pony. Go
on a Walk

Alexa's Favorites

Colors: Red Pink Purple yellow,

To Wear: Dress up stuff

Foods: Cheerios and Life cereal

Least Favorite to do: Fighting

TV show: Arthur, and Puppy Clifford

Snack: Fishy Crackers, Popcorn, Grapes

Computer game: Winnie the Pooh, Beauty and the Beast

Thing to do: Go to Kindergarten, and play with Brinley if she's nice

Favorites

CREATE YOUR OWN

Designing bold patterns using simple shapes effectively creates an original pattern without overpowering the layout. Follow the steps below to create your own patterned background paper. Create oversized tags for pictures using white and pink cardstock. Accent the tags with painted ribbon charms and pink ribbon. Print journaling in strips and attach them with pink brads.

Brandi Ginn

SUPPLIES: Pink, orange, blue and yellow cardstocks (Bazzill); chalk (Deluxe Designs); circle cutter or circle templates; ribbon charms, paint (Making Memories); chalk; ribbon; pink brads (Lasting Impressions); adhesive (Therm O Web)

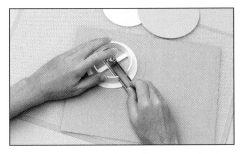

1 Cut various sized circles from several colors of cardstock with a circle cutter.

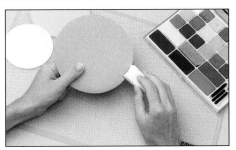

2 Chalk the edges of each circle with a makeup sponge.

3 Overlap circles and adhere to the background to create the pattern.

Wakeboard

DOUBLE-SIDED

Cut and fold letters across the middle of the page to reveal graphic double-sided paper. Print "Wakeboard" out on thin paper and adhere with temporary adhesive diagonally across page. Use a craft knife to cut out letters leaving the tops of the letters uncut. Score across uncut paper, at the top of the letters and fold back paper. Adhere folded page well with adhesive and glue centers of A, B, R and D to create mirror image of the word. Mount photo with large eyelets adding journaling on transparencies.

Pam Klassen
Photos: Ryan Watamura, Reedley, California

SUPPLIES: All patterned papers (Scrapworks); eyelets (Making Memories); adhesive (Therm O Web)

T**IP:** *Choose a font that has flat tops that will remain attached when the letters are cut out. There are many letter templates that work well for this technique.*

Criterium

COORDINATING

Add energy with coordinating graphic papers layered diagonally. Layer paper diagonally on background paper. Print title, cut out and adhere to filmstrip. Mount photos, print journaling and frame behind sticker. Add rub-on graffiti along angles in print and insert several eyelets.

Pam Klassen
Photos: Ryan Watamura, Reedley, California

SUPPLIES: Coordinating patterned paper and tag (Sassafras Lass); rub-on graffiti, eyelets (Creative Imaginations); adhesive (Therm O Web); filmstrip

E

ALTER

Graphic prints can easily be softened and texture added to the layout by using spray paint. Follow the step below to alter your background paper. Cut red cardstock and striped paper to 7 x 10"; ink the edges of cardstock and layer at angles on altered paper. Mat one photo on cream cardstock and adhere to the cardstock. Mat remaining photos over layered papers. Accent two sides of the design with brown ribbon and a decorative brad. Print the journaling using alphabet stamps and a black pen. Use a letter tile for the E.

Brandi Ginn

Photos: Nicci Irvine, Longmont, Colorado

SUPPLIES: Patterned paper (Mustard Moon); cardstock (Bazzill); Zig pen (EK Success); suede spray paint (Krylon); Versa Magic chalk ink (Tsukineko); ribbon (Offray); decorative brad (Making Memories); alphabet stamps (PSX Design); letter tile (Deluxe Designs); Super Tape adhesive (Therm O Web)

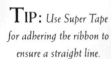

TIP: *Use Super Tape for adhering the ribbon to ensure a straight line.*

1 Spray patterned paper with a suede-textured spray paint.

Chapter SIX

Heritage photos are precious family treasures that reveal our history. Follow the ideas in this chapter and combine your black-and-white photos with beautiful patterned papers to create a page of quilt blocks, a coordinated two-page spread, heritage paper with stamps and paint, and aged paper with walnut ink. Several additional ideas will help you preserve the photos of your past.

Mimi & Ped

BACKGROUND

Frame a large heritage photo with vintage papers and accent with tags. Using coordinating patterned papers, lay a strip of 5" paper on left side of background. Cut a 5/8" photo frame and accent with 1/4" strips of paper, mount to page with photo corners. Print journaling on paper and adhere to tag. Pull ribbon and fiber from tags through punched hole on top of the page and adhere on back. Apply letter stickers and clip photo and leaf accent to ribbon.

Pam Klassen
Photos: Lori Pope, Reedley, California

SUPPLIES: Vintage patterned papers (Anna Griffin); dark blue patterned paper (Design Originals); letter stickers (K & Company); photo corners (Canson); tag (Avery); metal-rimmed tag (Creative Imaginations); leaf (Artchix Studio); metal clip (Scrapworks); adhesive (Therm O Web); 5/16" hole punch; ribbon

Heritage Variation

Creating a color scheme that blends with the photo then accenting next to the photo with a darker color creates an emphasis on the photo and keeps it the focal point of the page.

SUPPLIES: Background patterned paper (Daisy D's); script papers (7 Gypsies, K & Company); brown paper (Design Originals); letter stickers (K & Company); photo corners (Canson); tag (Avery); metal-rimmed tag (Creative Imaginations); leaf (Artchix Studio); metal clip (Scrapworks); adhesive (Therm O Web); 5/16" hole punch; ribbon

Pastel Variation

Extend the accent color beyond the photo frame by adding a torn piece of the accent color to the journaling block.

SUPPLIES: Patterned papers (Karen Foster Design); green paper (Pixie Press); letter stickers (K & Company); photo corners (Canson); tag (Avery); metal-rimmed tag (Creative Imaginations); leaf (Artchix Studio); metal clip (Scrapworks); adhesive (Therm O Web); 5/16" hole punch; ribbon

July 15, 1946

ACCENT

Tear patterned paper and adhere as a border along one side of black cardstock. Using clear photo corners, mount photos to teal cardstock and chalk the edges. Tear corners of patterned paper and use to accent under certain pictures. Embellish torn corners with photo anchors, eyelets and ribbon. Print the date on cream cardstock and cover with a bookplate laced with ribbon. Add paint to a metal plaque and quickly wipe away excess paint while wet.

Brandi Ginn
Photos: Helen Bryant, Aurora, Colorado

SUPPLIES: Patterned paper, photo anchors, eyelets, ribbon, bookplate, metal plaque (Making Memories); teal cardstock (Bazzill); chalk (Deluxe Designs); adhesive (Therm O Web)

Floral Pocket

EMBELLISHMENT

Trace a pocket template onto purple patterned paper. Cut floral paper to match the inside of the pocket and machine stitch in place. Fold sides to create pocket and secure with adhesive. Apply chalk to the edges of the pocket and embellish it with paper flowers, brads and trim.

Brandi Ginn

SUPPLIES: Purple patterned paper (Anna Griffin); floral paper (Rusty Pickle); pocket template, chalk (Deluxe Designs); paper flowers, brads (Making Memories); trim (found); adhesive (Therm O Web)

Envelope Variation

Trace an envelope template on patterned paper, fold and secure each side. Use acrylic paint and a foam stamp to embellish one corner of the envelope. Brush more paint along the edges and accent with metal washers and ribbon.

Brandi Ginn

SUPPLIES: Patterned paper (Me & My Big Ideas); envelope template (Deluxe Designs); Papier paint (Plaid); foam stamp, metal washers, ribbon (Making Memories); Memory Tape Runner adhesive (Therm O Web)

1 Trace an envelope shape using a template.

2 Score, fold and secure sides to create the envelope.

Jon and Kelly
BACKGROUND

Age-emboss paper background with metallic rub-ons. In honor of her father, Jon, Shannon created a loving memorial page. Cut the center from patterned paper. Rub embossed paper with metallic rub-ons to age. Cover paper with embossing ink and extra thick embossing enamel, melt with heat tool. Add center cardstock to background with foam spacers. Place strung beads above and below patterned paper. Mount photo off-center and add ribbons with charms. Stamp names on patterned paper and attach with ribbons.

Shannon Taylor, Bristol, Tennessee

SUPPLIES: Embossed patterned paper (K & Company); cardstock; ribbon words, ribbon charm (Making Memories); letter stamps (PSX Design); extra thick embossing powder (Ranger); metallic rub-ons (Craf-T); foam adhesive (Therm O Web); stringed beads

You Are My Past
MONOCHROMATIC

Tear papers in a mix of warm cream colors for a heritage background. Soften a precious photo with a mix of warm cream colors. Tear three papers to create a square on background paper. Color linen tape with ink and dry completely. Stick tape to center of page, sticking it to itself to create folds. Cut through layers to create openings for definition stickers. Cut music paper to frame photo. Adhere journaling to the frame with foam adhesives. Print title and embellish with vintage buttons and floral trim.

Pam Klassen
Photo: Angela Siemens, Rosenort, Manitoba, Canada

SUPPLIES: Background paper (Pebbles); button and script paper (K & Company); cream paper (Me & My Big Ideas); music paper (7 Gypsies); letter stickers (Colorbök); number stickers (Wordsworth); adhesive (Therm O Web); vintage buttons; floral trim (found)

TIP: *Remove backing on self-adhesive linen tape in short lengths when creating the folds.*

My Grandpa & Grandma

CREATE YOUR OWN

Create distinctive patterns using foam stamps and acrylic paint for an original design. Cut ¼" off each side of olive cardstock and adhere to maroon cardstock. Stitch in place using a machine and black thread. Follow the steps below to design your own patterned paper. Use handmade patterned paper to create a border on the left side. Place rivets at the top and bottom of the patterned paper; thread ribbon through each rivet. Secure the ribbon in back and tie a knot in front. Weave a ribbon charm through gingham ribbon, tie in the front and secure in back. Use black photo corners to secure main photo to maroon cardstock. Embellish a small file folder with a foam stamp and black paint. Place small, matted photos on the file folder. Create the title using rub-on letters and metal letters adhered with dimensional adhesive.

Brandi Ginn
Photos: Helen Bryant, Aurora, Colorado

SUPPLIES: Olive, maroon, brown cardstocks (Bazzill); foam stamps, ribbon charm, rub-on letters, metal letters (Making Memories); rivets (Chatterbox); Papier paint (Plaid); ribbon; file folder (Rusty Pickle); photo corners (Canson)

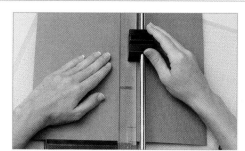

1 Cut brown cardstock to 4¾ x 12".

2 Stamp image onto cardstock using acrylic paint.

3 Once dry, lightly brush paint across the entire surface.

TIP: *When using scissors to silhouette cut flowers, keep your hand stationary, turning the paper to cut around petals.*

The Roe Girls

COORDINATING

Coordinate a two-page spread with silhouette cut floral frames and torn background. Tear two pieces of green vintage paper to cover the top of one page and the bottom of the second. Layer script paper on pages, one vertical and one horizontal. Cover two mat board frames with matching papers. Using small sharp scissors, silhouette cut opening in floral paper to surround the opening of the frame. Print and cut out title and mount on oval, add letter stickers. Adhere number stickers on squares. Accent with cut floral paper, vintage ribbon and buttons.

Pam Klassen
Photos: Lori Pope, Reedley, California

SUPPLIES: Green background paper (Chatterbox); green vintage, red vintage, floral paper (Anna Griffin); script paper (7 Gypsies); mat board frame kit (Papers by Catherine); number stickers (Wordsworth); letter stickers (Colorbök); adhesive (Therm O Web); ribbon, buttons

Jane Ann and Grandson

COORDINATING

Cut coordinating papers to quilt the background of a heritage page. Create 6" quilt squares for four corners of the page by cutting four rectangles 1¼ x 4¾"; adhere beside each other and border on two sides by 1¼ x 6" and 1¼ x 4¼" rectangles. Turn each 6" square a different direction. Mount photo on vintage fabric with photo corners. Place next to twill tape sticker and pin to vintage letter paper. Print title on script paper and pin to fabric. Sew on button and lace embellishment.

Pam Klassen
Photo: Lori Pope, Reedley, California

SUPPLIES: All patterned papers (Hot Off The Press); vintage letter papers (Me & My Big Ideas); letter stickers, twill ribbon (Pebbles); button (Junkitz); pins (Making Memories); adhesive (Therm O Web); lace, vintage kimono fabric (found)

TIP: *Lay quilt pieces on a cutting board with a grid to ensure consistent size of each quilt block.*

Generations Past

ALTER

Use walnut ink to alter patterned paper and create a vintage design. Create a vintage design by incorporating original techniques with tearing and stitching. Tear floral patterned paper along two sides and adhere to red cardstock. Follow the steps below to alter the patterned paper. Cut altered paper to a 10¼" square and layer on floral paper. Machine stitch a zigzag pattern along all sides of altered paper. Double mat photo on gray and red cardstocks using black photo corners; place in the center of the layout. For each ribbon detail, set two eyelets, weave ribbon and tie a knot on top. Use foam stamps and acrylic paint on canvas to create the main title, use woven letters for the remaining part of the title.

Brandi Ginn
Photo: Helen Bryant, Aurora, Colorado

SUPPLIES: Patterned paper (Deluxe Designs); red, gray cardstocks (Bazzill); photo corners (Canson); walnut ink; foam stamp (Rubber Stampede); sheer, gold-finish paint (Delta); foam letter stamps, eyelets (Making Memories); woven letters (Me & My Big Ideas); ribbon; Zots adhesive (Therm O Web)

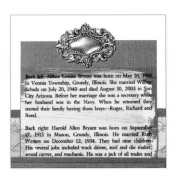

TIP: *When using walnut ink on patterned paper, there may be a tendency for the paper to warp. If this happens, simply use a warm iron to flatten the paper.*

1 Using a wet makeup sponge and watered down walnut ink, gently daub ink in a circular motion, covering the page. Work quickly to avoid splotches.

2 Paint a foam stamp with a more concentrated form of walnut ink and randomly stamp the image on the page.

3 Apply a sheer gold-finish paint with a makeup sponge to the entire page.

Chapter SEVEN

The holidays and seasons are a time of change, reflection and remembrance. Patterns that convey the season are in abundance, making the techniques used with these papers a focal point of this chapter. From rolling papers and using glaze to painting on canvas and creating with fabric, we have tried them all with great success. Be inspired by these uses of color and the ability to create texture throughout your own scrapbook pages.

Merry Christmas

BACKGROUND

Cut red patterned paper to 7" wide and layer on green patterned paper. Mount the main photo on green cardstock and adhere to red paper. To create the border of pictures, cut pieces of canvas into 3½" squares. Use black solvent ink to stamp canvas with a holly image and brush the edges of the canvas with red paint. Adhere pictures to the canvas with Super Tape and place on the page. Accent the border with woven words. To create the title, adhere a piece of twill tape with red brads to the top of the page. Chalk die-cut letters with red chalk and place on various metal-rimmed tags. Use jump rings and ribbon to secure the tags to the twill tape. Finish the title using rub-on words.

Brandi Ginn

SUPPLIES: Green patterned paper (Design Originals); red patterned paper (Lasting Impressions); green cardstock (Bazzill); solvent ink (Tsukineko); stamp (Hero Arts); cranberry paint, brads, tags, rub-on words (Making Memories); woven words, ribbon (Me & My Big Ideas); twill tape (Creek Bank Creations); chalk (Deluxe Designs); jump rings (Junkitz); adhesive (Therm O Web)

Slide Mount Variation

Frame pictures with slide mounts covered in patterned paper and use die-cut letters to create the title.

SUPPLIES: All patterned paper (Brother Sister Design Studio); red cardstock (Bazzill); slide mounts (Design Originals); die-cut letters (QuicKutz); adhesive (Therm O Web)

Metallic Variation

Accent photos with metal hinges and use word tiles to create the title.

SUPPLIES: Red patterned paper (Paper Patch); green patterned paper (Daisy D's); cream patterned paper (Li'l Davis Designs); red cardstock (Bazzill); chalk (Deluxe Designs); metal charm, page pebbles, eyelet hinges (Making Memories); ribbon (Me & My Big Ideas); printed tiles (Junkitz); adhesive (Therm O Web)

Thanksgiving

ACCENT

Accent a crisp fall page with template cut glazed leaves. Using a template and a thick black marker, draw leaves on patterned papers; cut leaves outside the black lines. Outline leaves with glaze, then fill centers, popping any bubbles. When completely dry, break glaze to flatten leaves and create a crumpled look. Use letter template to draw letters on bottom of photo mat, cut out with craft knife and back with accent paper. Adhere leaves, journaling and photo to page with brads.

Pam Klassen

Photo: Elizabeth Friesen, Reedley, California

SUPPLIES: Orange background, striped, plaid papers (Chatterbox); green, black cardstocks (Bazzill); letter template (Wordsworth); sepia glaze (Plaid); adhesive (Therm O Web); leaf template (source unknown), brads

Rolled Holiday Tree

EMBELLISHMENT

Revive an old-fashioned paper-rolling craft for the holidays. Use a variety of papers to cut 20 squares, each ¼" larger than the last. Follow the steps below to complete rolls and slide off dowel. Cut rolls to fit the base of the tree stem.

Pam Klassen

SUPPLIES: Patterned papers (Design Originals); cardstock (Bazzill); Gem-Tac liquid glue (Beacon Adhesives)

TIP: *Use a quick-drying, tacky glue to make this a quick and easy project.*

Holiday Variation

Use holiday-themed papers to create embellishments for any season, adding accents cut from solid cardstock.

Pam Klassen

SUPPLIES: Patterned papers (Design Originals); cardstock (Bazzill); Gem-Tac liquid glue (Beacon Adhesives)

1 Cut tree base shape and paper squares.

2 Put glue on the underside of one corner of square, start rolling paper square around dowel from opposite corner until roll is complete.

3 Glue rolled papers to base shape.

Spring
BACKGROUND

Use a background of color without overwhelming the photos. Cut a piece of blue patterned paper 9½ x 10¼" and mount on a patterned paper background. Cut three photos to fit within a piece of patterned paper cut 8¼ x 9⅛" and place on blue paper. Create the border along the bottom by tying gingham ribbon to each side of the page through an eyelet. Then embellish various tags and tiles with stickers and stamped letters. Attach the tags to the ribbon using jump rings and secure them in place with foam adhesive. To create the title, brush white acrylic paint on foam letter stamps and layer on background paper and blue paper.

Brandi Ginn
Photos: Kara Elmore, Kaysville, Utah

SUPPLIES: All patterned paper (Scrapworks); gingham ribbon (Offray); alphabet stamps (Hero Arts); word stickers (Bo-Bunny Press); tiles, jump rings (Junkitz); tags, acrylic paint, foam stamps (Making Memories); adhesive (Therm O Web)

Julia
MONOCHROMATIC

Piece together patterned papers to create the background. Mat all the photos on dark pink paper, extending the paper along one side of two photos. Using a file folder as a template, cut pink patterned paper into a photo mat. Adhere pink letters to the tab and place enlarged photo on top. Embellish the extending side of remaining photos with sticky mesh and rings stitched with embroidery floss and accented with pink ribbon. Print the journaling on white cardstock, cut into the shape of a tag and chalk the edges. Embellish the tag with a pink button and ribbon.

Brandi Ginn
Photos: Kara Elmore, Kaysville, Utah

SUPPLIES: Patterned paper (Scrapworks); pink flower paper (KI Memories); pink letters (Doodlebug Design); sticky mesh (Magic Mesh); rings (7 Gypsies); ribbon; chalk (Deluxe Designs); button (Junkitz); adhesive (Therm O Web)

Pickin' Pumpkins

Pickin' Pumpkins

CREATE YOUR OWN

Create original patterns using acrylic pain and canvas. Follow the steps below to create a brush-stroke pattern with natural colors inspired by those in the photos. Stitch painted canvas to green cardstock using a machine with a zigzag stitch and ink the edges of the cardstock. Mat all the photos on rust colored cardstock and adhere throughout the page. Accent two photos in the corner with torn pieces of script paper and a photo corner. Print the journaling on script paper and accent with various buttons. Paint a metal frame with acrylic paint and wipe away excess. To create the title, first print on white cardstock, then use a temporary adhesive to secure twill tape to the cardstock over the words and print again.

Brandi Ginn

SUPPLIES: Acrylic paint (DecoArt, Delta); cardstock (Bazzill); script paper (7 Gypsies); photo corners (Canson); Versa Magic chalk ink (Tsukineko); buttons, date tile (Junkitz); metal frame (Making Memories); twill tape (Creek Bank Creations); adhesive (Therm O Web)

1 Use a foam brush to apply a first layer of "brush stroke" stripes across canvas.

2 Repeat the process again, adding more color in brush strokes. Work quickly so colors blend easily before drying out.

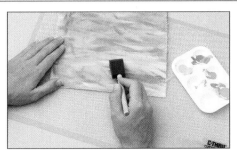

3 Go back over the canvas again, blending light and dark paint highlights covering the entire canvas.

American Baby

FABRIC

Use theme patterns found in fabrics to create an original background. Cut various fabrics and temporarily adhere to cream cardstock. Use a machine to stitch the fabric to the cardstock with a zigzag stitch. Ink the edges of exposed cream cardstock with blue chalk ink. Mat photos on red and cream cardstock and secure to the fabric with Super Tape. Create the title using red pebble letters and rubber stamps. Mat stamped letters on red cardstock and adhere with foam adhesive. Print journaling on cream cardstock, ink the edges and use Super Tape to adhere.

Brandi Ginn
Photos: David Mayes, Lafayette, Colorado

SUPPLIES: Fabric (Jo-Ann Fabric); cream and red cardstocks (Bazzill); chalk ink (Tsukineko); pebble letters (Li'l Davis Designs); alphabet stamps (Ma Vinci's Reliquary); Super Tape (Therm O Web)

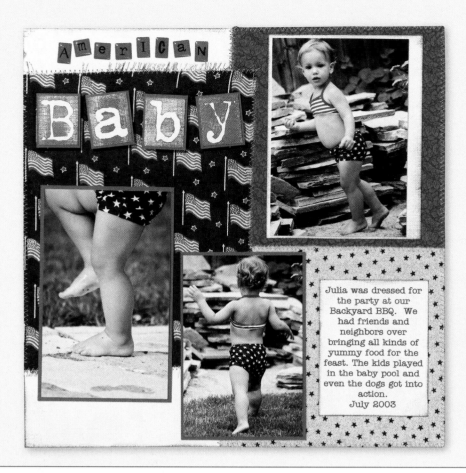

Julia was dressed for the party at our Backyard BBQ. We had friends and neighbors over bringing all kinds of yummy food for the feast. The kids played in the baby pool and even the dogs got into action.
July 2003

You two had fun running around over the holiday weekend. On Saturday we went to a friends house with a man-made lake where you were able to play in the water and chase after each other. Then on Sunday we watched the fireworks show from one of the nearby golf courses. Brinley lasted about 20 minutes and then she fell asleep!
July 2004

USA Girls

COORDINATING

Color blocks and accents add a touch of whimsy and patriotism to the design. Use a color-blocking card template to create and arrange squares and accents on the bottom right portion of blue cardstock. Highlight the squares by painting the edges with acrylic paint and embellishing with shaped buttons, tile letters, slide mounts and ribbon. Create the photo mat by stitching blue patterned paper to red cardstock using a zigzag stitch. Paint the edges of the photo mat and layer on an extended tag and squares. Fold up one corner of the blue cardstock, line with striped paper and accent with a star button. Place a swatch of red floral paper behind the blue cardstock to finish the page. Print journaling on white cardstock and adhere.

Brandi Ginn

SUPPLIES: All patterned paper, tile letters, shaped buttons (Doodlebug Design); red cardstock (Bazzill); red tiles (Little Black Dress Designs); Papier paint (Plaid); adhesive (Therm O Web)

American Pride

ALTER

Age red, white and blue paper squares by sanding them for a classic, time-worn, patriotic look. Punch out 1½" squares and then follow the instructions below to alter the squares. After mounting squares on cardstock, sand edges of photos and adhere on page. Cut quote sticker to fit on squares. Stamp title using dimensional paint and paint behind transparency to highlight journaling.

Pam Klassen

Photos: Ricki Helmsing, Phoenix, Arizona and Molly Bruce, Cave Creek, Arizona

SUPPLIES: Blue patterned papers (Hot Off The Press, K & Company, Karen Foster Design, Paper Patch); red patterned papers (Carolee's Creations, Chatterbox, Design Originals, K & Company, Magenta, Papers by Catherine); alphabet stamps (Ma Vinci's Reliquary); dimensional paint (Delta); quote sticker (Wordsworth); adhesive (Therm O Web)

THE LIFE GIVEN US
BY NATURE
IS SHORT, BUT
THE MEMORY
OF A *d...spent*
well.... *life*
IS ETERNAL
cicero

Macyn enjoying this years Fireworks
Display with friends, Tanner, Tristen
and Jacob. 2004

American Pride

TIP: *Use a grid ruler to line up squares for one row across the top and down the side of the layout. Fill in the remaining squares without a ruler.*

1 Punch squares from a variety of blue and red patterned papers.

2 Use sanding pad to sand all edges of squares and photos.

3 Adhere squares to page, spacing ¼" apart.

Chapter EIGHT

The special men that share your life may be 3 to 93. Use these ideas as inspiration to scrapbook the activities and interests of the important men in your life. Use a gutsy color combination, create patterned paper by combing Pattern Builder, make personalized stamps to alter your paper or use frame accents on a layout. There is a variety of additional ideas to inspire your masculine layouts.

Fishing

BACKGROUND

Sew textured paper and photos to a layout and create the rustic feel of the sport with the use of hemp fabric and netting. Adhere netting vertically down the center of the page. Cut rectangles of various papers, round outer corners and adhere to all corners of the layout. Layer ruler sticker, vellum journaling, fish sticker, photos and canvas title on top of papers. Machine stitch along each side of the netting through all thicknesses. Add a hook as an accent.

Pam Klassen

Photos: Pennie Stutzman, Broomfield, Colorado

SUPPLIES: Raffia patterned paper (Rusty Pickle); fish paper (K & Company); plaid paper (Scrapbook Wizard); camping supply list (Internet); rust cardstock (Bazzill); vellum (Treehouse Designs); mesh (Artchix Studio); hemp fabric (Creative Imaginations); ruler, fish sticker (K & Company); adhesive (Therm O Web); round corner punch, fish hook (found)

Geographical Variation

Pulling color inspiration for the patterned papers from the photos helps create continuity throughout the layout.

SUPPLIES: Olive green cardstock (Bazzill); striped, floral, linen papers (Chatterbox); map pattern paper (K & Company); vellum (Papers by Catherine); fish sticker (K & Company); mesh (Artchix Studio); hemp fabric (Creative Imaginations); twill word tape (source unknown); definition sticker (EK Success); adhesive (Therm O Web); round corner punch; fish hook (found)

All-American Variation

Use realistic textured patterned papers to continue the rustic outdoor feel of the layout.

SUPPLIES: Background paper (Daisy D's); linen paper (Pixie Press); bandanna paper (Wübie Prints); burlap paper (Sandylion); script paper (Papers by Catherine); vellum (DMD) mesh (Artchix Studio); hemp fabric (Creative Imaginations); fish sticker (K & Company) definition sticker (Making Memories); suede trim (Crafters Workshop); adhesive (Therm O Web); round corner punch, fish hook (found)

Dylan

ACCENT

Frame smaller photos or portions of photos with various slide mounts covered in patterned paper. Ink the edges of brown cardstock with black chalk ink. Mat photos on burgundy cardstock and ink the edges then layer one photo with a torn piece of paper. Cover an oversized slide mount and coin holder mount with various patterned papers and place over photos. Create the title using foam stamps and black paint and then accent the page with a woven letter.

Brandi Ginn

SUPPLIES: Patterned paper (Li'l Davis Designs); brown and rust cardstocks (Bazzill); chalk ink (Tsukineko); foam stamps, paint (Making Memories); woven letter (Me & My Big Ideas)

Adam & Mom

EMBELLISHMENT

Hinged embellishments can be created by attaching tags with jump rings for an interactive element on the page. Cut oversized tags and layer with torn pieces of patterned paper. Ink the edges of the paper with black chalk ink. Mat photos on rust colored cardstock and place throughout the tags. For a picture spanning two tags, first place the picture over both tags then cut in half with a craft knife. Use foam stamps and paint to create the large title and accent with metal stencil letters and die-cut letters.

Brandi Ginn

SUPPLIES: Patterned paper, metal stencil letters, pebble letters (Li'l Davis Designs); black and rust cardstocks (Bazzill); die-cut letters (Foofala); Versa Magic chalk ink (Tsukineko); jump rings; foam stamps, paint (Making Memories)

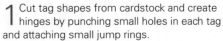

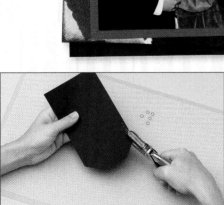

1 Cut tag shapes from cardstock and create hinges by punching small holes in each tag and attaching small jump rings.

'57 Chevy

BACKGROUND

Inspired by the red of the country barn, embellish a bandanna background. Cover mat board with paper and color with distress ink; emphasize the photo by matting with script paper. Color stencil letters with distress ink. Back first letter with background paper and use foam adhesive to mount on the layout, accent with nailheads. Color linen tape with distress ink to match letters, layer with sticker ribbon and small stencil letters. Use an old key and wood frame to imitate a buckle. Print journaling on tag and tie with torn bandanna.

Pam Klassen

Photo: Angela Siemens, Rosenort, Manitoba, Canada

SUPPLIES: Bandanna patterned paper, metal accent (K & Company); script paper, tag (7 Gypsies); letter stickers (EK Success); ribbon sticker (Pebbles); stencil letters (Ma Vinci's Reliquary); wood frame (Li'l Davis Designs); distress ink (Ranger); nailheads (Making Memories); foam adhesive, adhesive (Therm O Web); bandanna, keys (found)

TIP: *To print on a tag, print the text on paper, center and temporarily adhere the tag over text and reprint.*

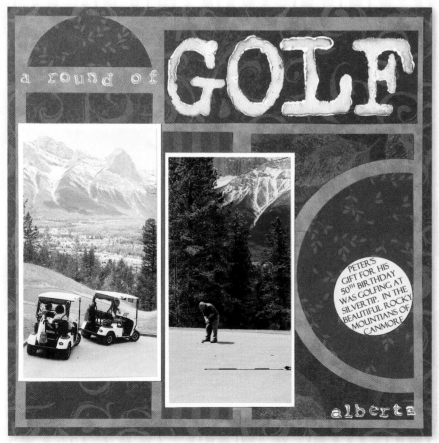

A Round of Golf

MONOCHROMATIC

Piece monochromatic papers to mimic the goal of the sport. Cut a slightly smaller paper to layer on top of the dark brown background. Using paint, stamp the title across the top of the layout. Cut strips of darker papers, and space apart across layout. Using a circle cutter, cut a circle out of far right paper strip, adding smaller circle inside. Create continuity with the circular shape above the title. Print journaling on white cardstock that resembles the golf ball.

Pam Klassen

Photos: Angela Siemens, Rosenort, Manitoba, Canada

SUPPLIES: Swirl, striped, small leaf pattern papers (Printworks); large leaf paper (Carolee's Creations); alphabet stamps (Ma Vinci's Reliquary, PSX Design); paint (Plaid); circle cutter or template; adhesive (Therm O Web)

A Boy's Will

CREATE YOUR OWN

Create an interesting textured background by combing with Pattern Builder—a paint-like gel medium that dries to an acrylic-like finish. Adhere a clear quote sticker near the bottom of cardstock background. Mix paint with Pattern Builder to create the desired color. Working on a protected surface, follow the directions below to create patterned paper. Let dry thoroughly. Trim edges and adhere to cardstock. Attach letter tiles to twill ribbon and wrap across layout. Sew label to photo and mount all photos, adding stickers.

Pam Klassen

Photos: Parry Klassen, Clovis, California

SUPPLIES: Cardstock (Bazzill); Pattern Builder, paint (Delta); letter and number stickers (Pebbles); label, tile letters, brads (Junkitz); twill ribbon (Offray); adhesive (Therm O Web)

1 Follow directions to mix paint with Pattern Builder until desired color is achieved. Use a palette knife to spread an even coat over entire page, except sticker.

2 While still wet, drag texture comb through colored Pattern Builder to create a design to fit the layout. Let dry completely.

TIP: *Don't worry about making a mistake when using Pattern Builder, just smooth it out and start over.*

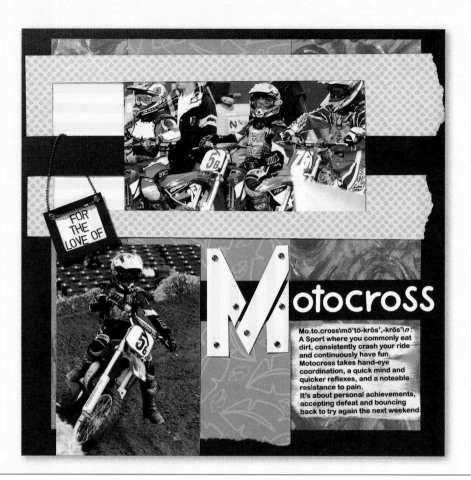

Motocross

GUTSY COLOR

Mimic the excitement and action of the sport through a layered mix of unusual colors. Cut two 1" strips of paper horizontally across page with a craft knife. Layer green paper over red and adhere under cut background pieces. Cut turquoise frame to fit photo, back with yellow paper and adhere behind top black strip. Add photo on top of black strip slipping edges under the frame. Use brads to mount stencil letter. Use eyelets and a chain to hang a small frame. Paint back of transparency to highlight definition journaling.

Pam Klassen
Photos: Ryan Watamura, Reedley, California

SUPPLIES: Red patterned paper (Carolee's Creations); green paper (Scrapbook Wizard); turquoise polka-dot and yellow striped paper (Printworks); black cardstock (Bazzill); stencil letter (Ma Vinci's Reliquary); letter stickers (KI Memories); paint (Plaid); chain (Making Memories); adhesive (Therm O Web); eyelets; brads

Guy's Weekend

COORDINATING

Layer papers and cut frames to showcase the photos of a fun weekend. Layer plaid and geometric papers across each other on striped background. Accent photo mat with solid papers and adhere to page with eyelets and jute. Create vertical frame by cutting four 2" square openings and accent with solid paper. Print journaling on vellum and tie below each opening with jute. Position photos on cardstock background under each opening; adhere frame with foam adhesive.

Pam Klassen
Photos: Ryan Watamura, Reedley, California

SUPPLIES: Coordinating patterned papers (Chatterbox); blue cardstock (Bazzill); vellum (DMD); acrylic accent (Junkitz); large eyelets (Making Memories); adhesive (Therm O Web); eyelets; jute

Determined

ALTER

Alter patterned paper with a custom-made foam stamp. Follow the steps below to alter patterned background paper. Mount two photos on a strip of blue cardstock and layer on patterned paper. Mat enlarged photo on red cardstock and staple a premade tab to the bottom right side. Print journaling on cardstock and place behind the enlarged picture; staple with a pull-tab for viewing. Create a border along the bottom by layering a zipper with black stitched ribbon and accent with a plastic letter. Cut strips of white paper and place letter stickers on each strip to create the title. Attach the title strips with staples and black brads.

Brandi Ginn
Photos: Kara Elmore, Kaysville, Utah

SUPPLIES: Patterned paper (Scrapworks); blue, white, red cardstocks (Bazzill); paint (Making Memories); premade tags, letter stickers (KI Memories); plastic letter (Deluxe Designs); zipper (Junkitz); ribbon; staples; brads (Lasting Impressions)

Imagine a two-year active little boy let loose on a farm! Wesley couldn't contain himself running from one thing to the next. I may have wanted him to go into the corn stalks but he was more than determined to get on that swing. He kept falling and slipping—we all had a hard time getting his skinny little body to balance by itself. Once he achieved his goal he couldn't have been happier.

He was so giddy running around he started to run and hide from Grandpa behind the trees. He couldn't stop laughing and his sweet little personality and characteristics were playful, blissful, and such a tease!

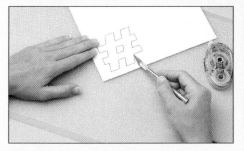

1 Print a pound sign image from the computer and attach with removable adhesive to foam paper to use as a pattern. Cut out foam with a craft knife.

2 Adhere the foam shape to a piece of foam core and paint with acrylic paint.

3 Stamp the image with red paint on patterned paper that has been brushed lightly with white acrylic paint.

Chapter NINE

The wonder of nature never ceases to inspire and amaze. Use the following ideas to help your layouts reflect the everyday wonders that surround you. Create patterned paper with color blocking and stamping, accent a letter stencil, use monochromatic squares to reflect a theme and fold back double-sided papers to create a photo mat. Use the additional ideas in this chapter to inspire your layouts with the amazing beauty around us.

Summer Flowers

BACKGROUND

Layer, slice and separate patterned papers across the layout to accent a year of the garden's beauty. Tear three strips from patterned papers; adhere next to each other to create a 4½" strip. Cut horizontally into ½" strips and spread ½" apart along left side of layout, occasionally covering handcut flower stem. Mat photos in coordinating paper. Stamp title into texture paint spread on hemp fabric. Pin stamped word to title and attach to page using buttons and jute. Print journaling on transparencies and adhere under strips and photo. Add transparencies and stickers under cut strips.

Pam Klassen

Photos: Angela Siemens, Rosenort, Manitoba, Canada

SUPPLIES: Background patterned paper, green paisley paper (Anna Griffin); script paper (7 Gypsies, Carolee's Creations); hemp fabric (Creative Imaginations); texture paint (Delta); alphabet stamps (Making Memories, PSX Design); mesh stamp (Magenta); transparencies (Artchix Studio); nature stickers (Pebbles); buttons, pin (Making Memories); adhesive (Therm O Web); jute

Contemporary Variation

Papers with a white background combined with coordinating buttons give this page a contemporary feel.

SUPPLIES: Background patterned paper (Autumn Leaves); floral paper (Carolee's Creations); script paper (Design Originals); hemp fabric (Creative Imaginations); texture paint (Delta); alphabet stamps (Making Memories, PSX Design); mesh stamp (Magenta); transparencies (Artchix Studio); buttons (Junkitz); adhesive (Therm O Web); jute; pin

Eclectic Variation

The eclectic combination of the definition paper and bright floral print creates a rustic but bold theme for this page.

SUPPLIES: Background patterned paper, word sticker (Pebbles); floral paper (Magenta); script paper (7 Gypsies, Rusty Pickle); hemp fabric (Creative Imaginations); texture paint (Delta); alphabet stamps (Making Memories, PSX Design); mesh stamp (Magenta); transparencies (Artchix Studio); clips (Making Memories); adhesive (Therm O Web); jute; staple

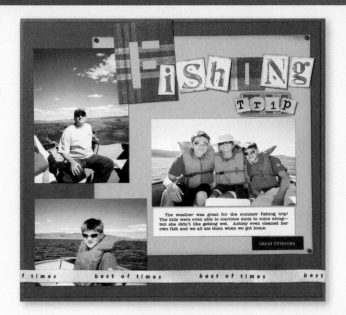

Fishing Trip

ACCENT

Accent with patterned-paper-covered letter stencils. Cut blue cardstock into an 11½" square; ink the edges with brown chalk ink and mount on green cardstock. Cut celery paper 8½ x 9¼"; ink the edges and attach with brads. Place photos throughout the layout and use printed twill tape as a border along the bottom. Cover a letter stencil with patterned paper and cut with a craft knife. Use alphabet stamps and chalk ink to create letters in the title. Place patterned paper inside a rectangle tag and cover with pebble letters. Accent the enlarged photo mat with a woven word.

Brandi Ginn

Photos: Nancy Collings, Farmington, Utah

SUPPLIES: Patterned paper (Deluxe Designs); blue, green, celery cardstocks (Bazzill); chalk ink (Tsukineko); twill tape, letter stencils (7 Gypsies); brad, rectangle tag (Making Memories); alphabet stamps (Ma Vinci's Reliquary); letter pebbles (Creative Imaginations); woven label (Me & My Big Ideas); adhesive (Therm O Web)

TIP: *To give an aged look to the printed twill tape, use a makeup sponge and blot the tape with brown chalk ink.*

Gone Fishing

EMBELLISHMENT

Create a custom frame using patterned papers and slide mounts. Cover enlarged slide mounts with patterned paper following the steps below. Rub the edges of covered slide mounts with brown chalk ink. Tie slide mounts together with brown ribbon and use to frame title and photo blocks. Use die-cut letters to create the title and date. Accent with pre-made slide mounts rubbed with ink and brown tiles.

Brandi Ginn

Photos: Nancy Collings, Farmington, Utah

SUPPLIES: Patterned paper, premade slide mounts (Deluxe Designs); slide mounts (Design Originals); Versa Magic chalk ink (Tsukineko); ribbon (Offray); die-cut letters (QuicKutz); tiles (Little Black Dress Designs); Memory Tape Runner and Super Tape adhesives (Therm O Web)

1 Using paper slightly larger than the slide mount, cut each corner at angles and cut an X in the middle of the mount.

2 Fold all sides of the paper to wrap around the slide mount and secure with adhesive.

Tornado
BACKGROUND

Use a background paper that continues the movement created in the photographs. Complement photos by their placement on the background paper. Adhere letter stickers on transparency for the title and bend journaling using a word-processing or page-design software program, printing onto transparency. Roughly paint under transparencies with white paint, let dry and adhere to page by placing adhesives under painted areas.

Pam Klassen
Photos: Angela Siemens, Rosenort, Manitoba, Canada

SUPPLIES: Blue striped patterned paper, letter stickers (Wordsworth); paint (Delta); adhesive (Therm O Web)

Winter Silence
MONOCHROMATIC

Build a mood with monochromatic color blocks. Sue creates a serene feeling by duplicating the blues of her photos with her papers. Double-layer cardstock, then cut 1¼" squares from blue patterned papers, spacing them evenly to fill empty spaces around the photos. Handcut the title and highlight the metal accents with metallic rub-ons and glaze; adhere with a ribbon.

Sue Thomas, Anoka, Minnesota

SUPPLIES: Background cardstock (Bazzill); blue patterned papers (Creative Imaginations, Paper Adventures, Scrap Ease); molding strip, paints, metallic rub-ons (Making Memories); snowflake charm (Tin-Tiques); ribbon

Estes Park

CREATE YOUR OWN

Using basic stamped shapes and coordinating colors, you can easily create simple patterned backgrounds. Follow the steps below to create the patterned paper background. Mat photos on brown cardstock and place throughout the design. Using a machine, accent photo mats with a zigzag stitch. Place rivets on opposite corners of one photo and use to anchor tied gingham ribbon. Create the title using premade letters and die-cut letters. Print journaling on a transparency and adhere with a spray adhesive.

Brandi Ginn

SUPPLIES: All cardstocks (Bazzill); leaf stamp (Hero Arts); watermark inkpad (Tsukineko); rivets (Chatterbox); ribbon; premade letters (Foofala); die-cut letters (QuicKutz); transparency (Grafix); spray adhesive (Creative Imaginations); Memory Tape Runner adhesive (Therm O Web)

TIP: *Make sure that the stamp is loaded with ink and press the image firmly on a flat surface to ensure the entire design is transferred.*

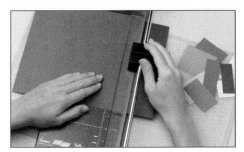

1 Cut colors of coordinating cardstock in various sized rectangles and squares.

2 Working from left to right, adhere the shapes to a 12 x 12" piece of cardstock.

3 Stamp a leaf image throughout the design using a watermark inkpad.

Explore Nature

DOUBLE-SIDED

Fold back the corners of four double-sided papers to reveal the wonders of nature. Use temporary adhesive and plenty of working space to lay out four 12 x 12" double-sided papers with corners touching in the center. Measure 2½" from each corner, score across paper and fold back, creating square opening for photo. Adhere opening off center on background paper, mounting photo, trim edges to fit page. Create openings for nature stickers by cutting 1¼" plus signs (+) directly into patterned paper; fold back two corners and place edges of stickers beneath folded corners. Adhere preprinted and computer printed fabrics to page then punch evenly spaced holes for threading jute, tying at the corners of the page. Add stamped tags and leaf sticker.

Pam Klassen

Photo: Angela Siemens, Rosenort, Manitoba, Canada

SUPPLIES: Patterned papers (Bisous); nature stickers (Bisous, Pebbles); hemp fabric (Creative Imaginations); canvas phrase (Li'l Davis Designs); adhesive (Therm O Web); jute

TIP: *Punching holes anywhere on a layout through several thicknesses is possible using a hammer and an eyelet hole punch on top of a cutting mat.*

Our Backyard Bugs

COORDINATING

Layer and accent coordinating papers in natural tones. Tarri creates a feeling of wonder with close-up photos of insects against a coordinating background. Layer coordinating strips of three different papers horizontally across the layout, separating with premade borders. Stamp the title and soften it with paint to blend with the coordinating stickers and papers. Use the empty space in the photos to add journaling and accent with a magnifying glass.

Tarri Botwinski, Grand Rapids, Michigan

SUPPLIES: Patterned paper, tags, tacks, letter stickers, rub-ons (Chatterbox); foam stamps (Making Memories); paint (Delta); magnifying glass

Eat Sand

ALTER

A watery background is created using patterned paper to complement beach photos. Follow the steps below to create the patterned-paper background. Print definition journaling on strips of white cardstock and chalk the edges. Place strips around the outside edges of the design and secure with a zigzag stitch. Mount photos with white photo corners randomly throughout the page. Accent with seashell zipper pull, jump ring and ribbon attached to one picture. Use solvent ink and alphabet stamps to print "sand" on a zipper pull. Create title and caption using die-cut letters, slide mount, zipper pull, jump ring, ribbon, watch face and watch crystal. Print journaling on a transparency and paint the back with acrylic paint.

Brandi Ginn

SUPPLIES: Patterned paper (Karen Foster Design); yellow and white cardstocks (Bazzill); photo corners (Canson); zipper pulls, jump rings (Junkitz); die-cut letters (QuicKutz); ribbon (Making Memories); StazOn solvent ink (Tsukineko); alphabet stamps (EK Success); Perfect Paper adhesive (USArtQuest); transparency (Grafix); paint (Making Memories); spiral clip (7 Gypsies)

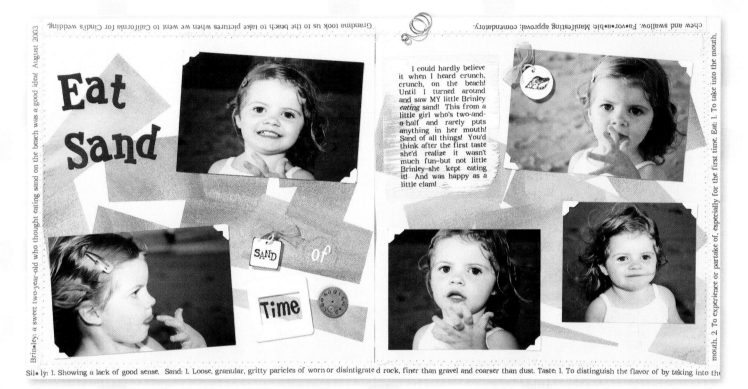

TIP: *After applying adhesive, it is helpful to smooth out the paper with a brayer.*

1 Cut random angular shapes from patterned paper using a paper trimmer.

2 Arrange on yellow cardstock.

3 Adhere with Perfect Paper adhesive.

Chapter TEN

Kindergarten through high school are our children's most formidable years and they pass so quickly. Relive those school-year memories by creating layouts using the ideas in the following pages. Create a coin holder embellishment, use team colors for inspiration, create patterned paper with stamps and alter a paper with paint and a screen. The additional ideas in this chapter will inspire you to capture those childhood memories.

High School

BACKGROUND

Cut a school folder and collage with the busy year of a high school student. Cut cardstock to create the front flap of a school folder. Use papers that contrast with the background to cover folder flap, adding stickers. Adhere flap to the side of the background page with eyelets. Mount photos on cardstock and distress by rolling and inking edges, adhere to layout with clips. Cut photo to cover top of photo slide frame and mount over an enlarged photo. Stamp title with paint and add paint behind journaling printed on a transparency.

Pam Klassen
Photos: Wayne Wiebe, Reedley, California

SUPPLIES: Background patterned paper (Rusty Pickle); number paper (Carolee's Creations); map patterned paper (Design Originals); orange cardstock (Bazzill); definition, letter sticker, twist tie (Pebbles); ruler sticker (K & Company); alphabet stamps (Ma Vinci's Reliquary); paint (Plaid); slide mount, metal clip (Scrapworks); snaps (Chatterbox); photo anchors (Making Memories); adhesive (Therm O Web); eyelets

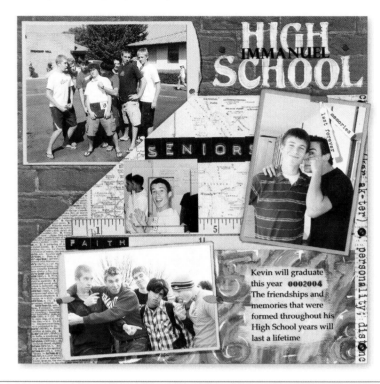

Energetic Variation

Capture the energy of the senior year by creating a title with ransom lettering from alphabet paper combined with rub-on lettering. Mat photos in bright red.

SUPPLIES: Background patterned paper (Wordsworth); alphabet paper (Rusty Pickle); map paper (Design Originals); circle paper (SEI); green cardstock (Bazzill); definition, letter stickers (Pebbles); ruler sticker (K & Company); rub-on letters (Autumn Leaves); letter stickers (Creative Imaginations); wood frame (Li'l Davis Designs); elastic bands, clip (7 Gypsies); adhesive (Therm O Web); eyelets

Contemporary Variation

Using pure white as the background color in this layout makes the photos and journaling pop off the page. The variety of fasteners, used to attach photos to the page, gives a contemporary feel.

SUPPLIES: Background patterned paper (Carolee's Creations); number and definition paper (7 Gypsies); small and large letter paper (Karen Foster Design); letter stickers (Wordsworth); rub-on graffiti (Creative Imaginations); die-cut letters (QuickKutz); acrylic frame (Heidi Grace Designs); twist tie (Pebbles); clip (Making Memories); adhesive (Therm O Web); eyelets; staples

Pee Wee Soccer

ACCENT

Accent the design with folded tabs set with eyelets. Mat photos on red and yellow cardstocks; create oversized mats for various photos. Apply rub-on words to the extended portion of the photo mat. Cut strips of patterned paper ¾ x 2", fold in half around photo mats and set with a red eyelet. Thread string through tabs and secure in eyelets set in the corners. Use foam stamps, acrylic paint and die-cut letters to create the title.

Brandi Ginn

SUPPLIES: Patterned paper (SEI); blue, red, yellow and white cardstocks (Bazzill); rub-on words, foam stamps, acrylic paint, eyelets (Making Memories); die-cut letters (QuicKutz); adhesive (Therm O Web)

Go Girl

EMBELLISHMENT

Alter a coin holder for a unique frame embellishment. Layer patterned and solid papers over a coin holder; age papers slightly with sandpaper. Embellish each hole with pictures and accents. To create a page pebble over the date, first stamp the date on orange paper and fill the circle with liquid dimensional adhesive and let dry. Paint a metal letter and attach it with jump rings and ribbon.

Brandi Ginn

SUPPLIES: Patterned paper (SEI); alphabet stamps (Hero Arts); Versa Color ink (Tsuki-neko); metal letter (Making Memories); acrylic paint (Delta); jump rings (Junkitz); ribbon (Offray); word dot (Creative Imaginations); adhesive (Therm O Web)

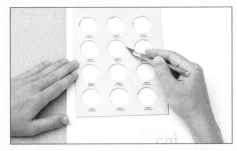

1 Trace the circles from a coin holder on the back of patterned paper. Keep the coin holder in place and cut out circles carefully with a craft knife.

Water Polo

BACKGROUND

Choose background paper inspired by the shape of the ball and the feel of the water. Mat photos over layered blocks of coordinating paper. Continue the paper design with circular acrylic accents strung on a black fiber and adhered on the back of the page through eyelets. Self-adhesive acrylic letters reflect the wet feeling of the water.

Pam Klassen

Photos: Ryan Watamura, Reedley, California

SUPPLIES: Background patterned paper (Li'l Davis Designs); striped patterned paper (SEI); acrylic letters, accents (Heidi Grace Designs); adhesive (Therm O Web); eyelets; fiber

First Year of School

MONOCHROMATIC

Layer and stitch a combinaton of red papers. Cover three quarters of the background paper with number paper and zigzag stitch down two edges. Tear small plaid paper in half, place across center of page and use a straight stitch across both edges. Mount photos and stickers, insert eyelets and tie ribbon around photos. Outline die-cut letters with a pen and adhere to lined school paper. Print journaling on the lined paper and adhere under edges of papers.

Pam Klassen

Photos: MaryAnn Klassen, Reedley, California

SUPPLIES: Numbered patterned paper (7 Gypsies); large plaid paper (Daisy D's); small plaid paper (Provo Craft); photo stickers (Pebbles); die-cut letters (Quic-Kutz); ribbon (Artchix Studio); eyelets (JewelCraft); adhesive (Therm O Web)

TIP: *Various colors of cardstock absorb inks differently. For example, the reddish color used on this layout is actually called "Bark" and looks brown on the inkpad. Use a small stamp on scrap pieces of cardstock to test how certain colors will look.*

Preschool Graduate

CREATE YOUR OWN

Create patterned paper using stamps, chalk ink and textured paper. Tear one side of polka-dot paper and ink the edges with chalk ink. Use a zigzag stitch to adhere the paper to yellow cardstock. Follow the steps below to create stamped paper; layer over background paper. Double mat the main photo on blue and green cardstocks with inked edges and one torn side. Layer stamped title over blue and green cardstocks and finish the title by stamping on a premade tag. Create picture and journaling tags by layering various colors of cardstock and use a machine to stitch them together; accent with ribbon.

Brandi Ginn

SUPPLIES: Polka-dot paper, premade tag, nails (Chatterbox); yellow, olive, blue and rust cardstocks (Bazzill); alphabet stamps (Ma Vinci's Reliquary, PSX Design); Versa Magic chalk ink, Versa Color ink (Tsukineko); Colorbox brown chalk ink (Clearsnap); ribbon

1 Cut two sheets of cream-colored, textured cardstock into 9 x 8" rectangles.

2 Begin stamping the alphabet with chalk finish inkpads.

3 Continue stamping until the entire surface is covered.

Soccer Dreams

INSPIRATION

Create a color scheme inspired by team uni-forms and colors of the field. Trim red crackle paper and layer over green script background. Cut through both layers with a craft knife creating two vertical strips 3/8 x 5". Layer black definition paper over striped paper and slide through cut section of paper. Top small photo with acrylic frame, and adhere transparency title to page with strips of paper. Add rub-on phrase and letter stickers for journaling.

Pam Klassen

Photos: Pennie Stutzman, Broomfield, Colorado

SUPPLIES: Background patterned paper (Karen Foster Design); striped paper (Me & My Big Ideas); red crackle paper (Paper Adventures); definition paper (Pebbles); transparency letters (Carolee's Creations); letter stickers (Wordsworth); letters (Scrapworks); rub-on graffiti (Creative Imaginations); acrylic frame (Heidi Grace Designs); adhesive (Therm O Web)

First Day

COORDINATING

Layer and sew coordinating school papers. Tarri creates a special memory of her son's first day of school. Layer strips of papers on the back-ground; machine stitch the centerpiece and ac-cent with striped paper along the edge. Stitch the darker patterned paper along the bottom to highlight the pictures, adding letter stickers and journaling on tags. Highlight a backpack with a circular frame.

Tarri Botwinski, Grand Rapids, Michigan

SUPPLIES: Patterned paper, I.D. tags, tacks, letter stickers, frame, rivets, nails (Chatterbox)

Soccer

ALTER

Use a metal screen and acrylic paint to change the appearance of the patterned paper. Frame red cardstock on three sides with black cardstock; repeat for the other side of the layout so there is no black in the center. Follow the steps below to create altered paper. Cut altered paper in three strips. Mount on black cardstock and place on the left side of the design. Use various portions of two color-blocking templates to design the photo placement. Highlight a portion of one picture by framing with a punched square frame. Print the mirror image of a computer font and cut from black cardstock with a craft knife to create the title. Add die-cut letters for name.

Brandi Ginn

SUPPLIES: Patterned paper (Rusty Pickle); red and black cardstocks (Bazzill); color-blocking templates (Deluxe Designs); acrylic paint, brads (Making Memories); square punch; die-cut letters (QuickKutz); adhesive (Therm O Web)

TIP: *Combine designs from two color-blocking templates to create one design.*

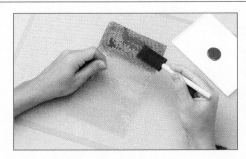

1 Apply acrylic paint to the surface of a metal screen with a sponge brush, allowing the paint to fill the holes.

2 Starting at the top left side of the paper, tap the screen with your finger to transfer the paint.

3 Apply more paint to the screen and continue tapping until the page is covered. Allow to dry and then cut.

Chapter ELEVEN

We all have photos of those touching moments where life makes you stop and remember what is important. In these cases, traditional journaling just isn't enough to convey the mood and is replaced with quotes, captions or family sentiments. Papers can also affect the tone of the design. Each piece of artwork below works with the photos used but the colors and patterns each lend a unique feel to the page. Discover fun ways to use patterned paper to express your emotions in this chapter.

Families Are Forever

BACKGROUND

Stitch together bold patterns and warm, rich colors to create a striking canvas for family photos. Adhere patterned papers to cardstock and machine stitch zigzag pattern. Use foam stamps, acrylic paint and rub-on letters to create the title. Accent with printed twill tape and a metal ring.

Brandi Ginn

SUPPLIES: Red patterned paper (Wordsworth); script paper (Rusty Pickle); cardstock (Bazzill); twill tape (7 Gypsies); ring (Li'l Davis Designs); foam alphabet stamps, acrylic paint, rub-on letters (Making Memories)

Cool Variation

Create a design using a cool color scheme and contrasting accents.

SUPPLIES: Blue patterned paper, letter stickers (Wordsworth); script paper (7 Gypsies); green and black cardstocks (Bazzill); foam alphabet stamps (Making Memories); pebble letters (Li'l Davis Designs); ribbon (Me & My Big Ideas); buttons (Junkitz)

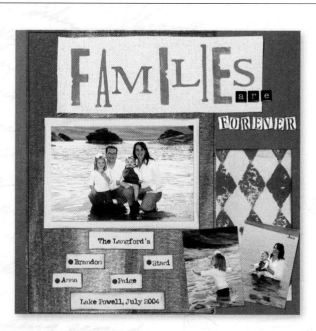

Saturated Variation

Use deep-colored, nature-inspired paper colors and cheery argyle patterns to complement the photos.

SUPPLIES: Green patterned paper (Wordsworth); diamond paper, pebble letters (Li'l Davis Designs); green and yellow cardstocks (Bazzill); brads (Lasting Impressions); letters (Foofala); foam alphabet stamps, acrylic paint (Making Memories)

Garden Fairy

ACCENT

Tear patterned paper across page to reveal a timid garden fairy. Cut ½" pink frame to fit the edge of pale green cardstock background. Print title vertically across patterned paper with word art program. Adhere to the left side of layout and tear away across page. Stamp wings on vellum using watercolor markers, cut out and attach to silhouetted photo. Tuck photo and wings partially behind patterned paper and frame. Add sticker flowers to edge of paper and hat. Tear a dark green border strip. Thread glass beads on embossing thread and string across border, topping with brad stickers. Add name with letter stickers.

Pam Klassen
Photo: Richard Gerbrandt, Reedley, California

SUPPLIES: Patterned paper (Bisous); pale pink, pale green and dark green cardstocks (Bazzill); floral stickers (Magenta); letter stickers (SEI); brad stickers (Scrapbook Wizard); wing stamp (Alextamping); watercolor markers (EK Success); glass leaf beads (Artchix Studio); adhesive (Therm O Web); embossing floss

Sentiment on a String

EMBELLISHMENT

Cut and layer letter sticker circles. String letters together to create a sweet sentiment. Follow the steps below to create the embellishment. Add sticker letters to a tag and attach it to the tassel end of the cord.

Pam Klassen

SUPPLIES: Red patterned paper (Anna Griffin); striped, red leaf papers (Diane's Daughters); letter stickers (Chatterbox, K & Company); tassel (Provo Craft); Memory Tape Runner and Super Tape adhesives (Therm O Web); eyelets

TIP: *When mounting this embellishment on a layout, position it under a cut-out opening in the page protector so it can be easily opened.*

Baby/Child Variation

Using cute, contemporary papers and layered squares, create a sentiment for a child or baby.

Pam Klassen

SUPPLIES: Patterned papers (KI Memories); letter stickers (SEI); adhesives (Therm O Web); ribbon; eyelets

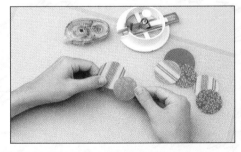

1 Use circle cutter to cut nine 1⅝" circles, nine 1⅞" circles, two 2" and two 2¼" circles. Adhere smaller circles to the centers of larger circles.

2 Punch ⅜" holes ½" apart at the top of circles. Hammer eyelets into holes on front and back covers.

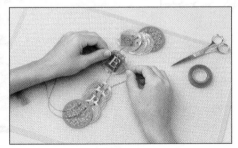

3 Line up letters to form words from top to bottom with front and back covers in place. Wrap cord with tape near tassel and cut through tape. Run cut end through right hole on front cover, through each letter circle and back cover. Secure end to back with tape. Repeat with second cord through left hole.

Dare to Dream
BACKGROUND

Bold blues and purples found in the patterned paper are a striking complement to the black-and-white photo. Mat photo on purple cardstock and set three eyelets in the upper left-hand corner. Thread several shades of ribbon through the eyelets and tie together with ribbon. Mount picture on foam core and place on the bottom right side of the patterned paper. Use rub-on letters to create the title. Print journaling on a transparency and adhere under the photo mat.

Brandi Ginn

SUPPLIES: Patterned paper (Wordsworth); purple cardstock (Bazzill); eyelets (Creative Imaginations); ribbon; rub-on words (Making Memories); transparency (Grafix); adhesive (Therm O Web)

Wesley
COORDINATING

Use coordinating patterns to create a balanced design. Cut patterned papers at angles and ink the edges with brown chalk ink. Adhere to blue cardstock and machine stitch in place. Ink the outside edges of the layout. Crumple, ink and tear patterned paper along one side to create part of the photo mat. Adhere the picture to celery cardstock; ink the edges and mount on foam core. Mount foam core to crumpled paper and place on page. Use alphabet stamps and chalk ink on a premade stitched envelope. Accent the envelope with rivets, ribbon and painted metal numbers and letters. Create the title using die-cut letters and ink the edges with chalk ink.

Brandi Ginn
Photo: Kara Elmore, Kaysville, Utah

SUPPLIES: Patterned paper, rivets, premade envelope (Chatterbox); alphabet stamps (Wordsworth); chalk ink (Tsukineko); wide ribbon (Offray); metal accents, thin ribbon (Making Memories) die-cut letters (QuicKutz); adhesive (Therm O Web)

I took a moment from my daily tasks and watched you. In the smallest detail you take delight. All that you experience captures your imagination.

I learned from you today.

TIP: *Self-adhesive mosaic tiles are easy to decorate with stamps, stickers, inks and colored pencils.*

You Inspire Me

CREATE YOUR OWN

Create patterned paper with the soft look of tiles by chalking and embossing precut adhesive paper. Follow the steps below, repeating the ink, powder and heating to create a smooth surface. Cover right side of the layout with mosaic tiles and mount photo on the left side. Adhere quote sticker on embossed mat and mount on tiles. Die cut title letters and machine stitch to title border. Stamp remaining title and adhere to the bottom of page with eyelets and clip.

Pam Klassen

Photo: Ryan Watamura, Reedley, California

SUPPLIES: Mosaic adhesive sheet (Magenta); blue cardstock (Bazzill); chalk (Deluxe Designs); quote sticker (Wordsworth); decorative clip (source unknown); embossing ink (Tsukineko); extra thick embossing powder (Ranger); alphabet stamps (Ma Vinci's Reliquary); adhesive (Therm O Web); pompom; alligator clip; eyelets

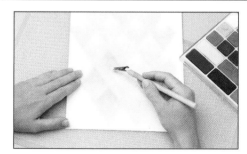

1 Use alligator clip and mini pompom to apply light blue chalk to top of each mosaic and purple chalk on the bottom. Blend colors in the centers.

2 Rub embossing ink over entire surface of chalked mosaic sheet. While still wet, cover with extra thick embossing powder. Melt powder with heat gun and repeat.

3 Fold mosaic along precut lines and remove from paper backing. Space diamonds evenly ⅛" apart; trim excess from page edges.

silly · cute

funny · smart · kind

tons to sing and talk

sister, daughter, friend

Jun

2003

Brinley

INSPIRATION

Be inspired by shabby chic techniques like sanding, crumpling and stitching. Using a fine-grit sandpaper, gently rub across the background cardstock. Crumple various striped patterned papers and smooth flat. Create a 2½" border with a large strip of paper. Create photo mats by mounting smaller striped paper at angles on purple paper and orange floral paper; machine stitch in place and place on layout. Create the title using die-cut letters and layering a premade frame on a tag. Print journaling on a transparency and paint the back with acrylic paint. Accent the design with coordinating buttons.

Brandi Ginn

SUPPLIES: Patterned paper, premade frame (Chatterbox); die-cut letters (QuickKutz); tag template (Deluxe Designs); buttons (Junkitz); acrylic paint (Delta); adhesive (Therm O Web)

Cherish Families

MONOCHROMATIC

Enhance photos by creating a monochromatic color scheme. Layer a 1½" strip of blue cardstock on dark blue cardstock. Using a machine, sew a zigzag stitch across the seam made by the blue cardstock. Layer pieces of light blue cardstock, floral and polka-dot papers; mount photo on top.
Cut two tags from blue plaid paper and place under light blue cardstock as a decorative element, embellish with painted washers and white ribbon. Adhere blue ribbon across the top of the design and string stamped tags on a metal chain strung through eyelets and secure in back. Create the title using rub-on words over patterned paper and photo.

Brandi Ginn
Photo: Brian Cummings, Aliso Creek, California

SUPPLIES: Floral patterned paper (KI Memories); polka-dot, plaid papers (Lasting Impressions); blue cardstock (Bazzill); washers, tags, stamps, metal chain, ribbon, rub-on words (Making Memories); stamping ink (Hero Arts); acrylic paint (Plaid); adhesive (Therm O Web)

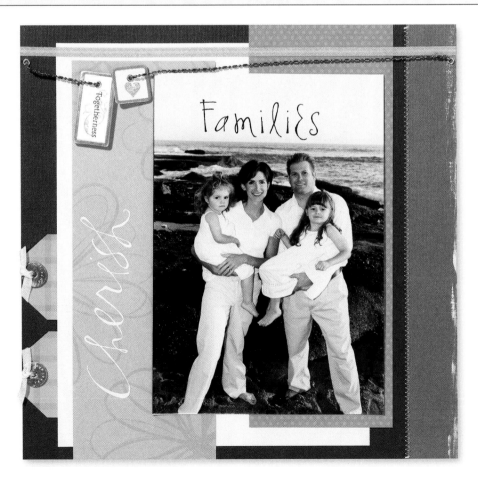

Togetherness

Families

Cherish

Cherish

ALTER

Change the theme of the paper by cutting slots and inserting sentimental hearts. Follow the steps below to create hearts and alter the background paper. Mark placement of hearts on patterned paper and remove. After machine stitching edges of blue patterned paper to cardstock, slide hearts through cut slots and adhere to page. Print journaling on top of vellum, stamp title on bottom and back with torn white paper; add quote sticker. Adhere vellum to layout behind the photo. Hang charms from cardstock strip secured across paper.

Pam Klassen

Photo: Angela Siemens, Rosenort, Manitoba, Canada

SUPPLIES: Blue patterned paper (Heidi Grace Designs); red script paper (7 Gypsies); cardstock (Bazzill); vellum (Autumn Leaves); alphabet stamps (Ma Vinci's Reliquary); quote sticker (Karen Foster Design); chain (Making Memories); charms (Hirschberg Schutz & Co.); adhesive (Therm O Web)

TIP: *Create a variation of this technique by inserting leaf shapes into nature-themed paper or stars into a Christmas pattern.*

1 Trace stencil hearts on back of patterned paper; cut out hearts.

2 Mark placement of hearts on patterned paper. Use craft knife to cut strips the width of hearts across paper.

3 Machine stitch edges of blue paper to cardstock. Slide hearts into cut slits and adhere to page.

Chapter TWELVE

Looking back on your travels—from the yearly trip to visit relatives to the once-in-a-lifetime trip to a foreign country—is easy when you keep your travel memories alive using the ideas in this chapter. Collage and stitch themed paper, use a variety of patterned paper accents, create a small travel book embellishment and tear back double-sided paper for a photo opening. Use the additional ideas in this chapter to fit your travel theme.

Fun by the Sea

ACCENT

Cut photo windows on an angle to create interest and accent with an illuminated letter. Tear two patterned papers and mat in the center of background paper. Cut windows diagonally in 5½" wide paper. Accent the edges of frame with darker paper. Conceal journaling by placing hinges along one side of matted frame. Print title on vellum and adhere beneath diagonal opening. Wrap large letter with fiber, tie on a tag stamped with words and embellish with glitter. Place ribbon across page, securing with an inked stone embellishment.

Pam Klassen

Photos: Gayelynn Duggan, Morrison, Colorado

SUPPLIES: Painted wood paper (Me & My Big Ideas); blue wash paper (Wordsworth); map paper (Design Originals); compass paper (K & Company); pastel squares paper (Rusty Pickle); explore sticker (NRN Designs); definition sticker (Pebbles); travel sticker, hinges (Making Memories); tag (DMD); ribbon (Artchix Studio); alphabet stamp (PSX Design); stone (Clearsnap); glitter (DecoArt); adhesive (Therm O Web)

Vintage Travel Variation

The use of vintage-style papers, font and embellishments gives this layout a rustic feel.

SUPPLIES: Background patterned paper (Scrap Ease); photo paper (Rusty Pickle); map and compass paper (K & Company); vintage paper (Anna Griffin); script paper (7 Gypsies); travel sticker (Making Memories); letter stickers (Pebbles); tag (DMD); tassel (Provo Craft); ribbon, metal ring (Artchix Studio); alphabet stamp, hinges (Making Memories); adhesive (Therm O Web)

Contemporary Variation

Fun bright papers and a white background help pull together a contemporary look.

SUPPLIES: Striped background, polka-dot patterned paper (KI Memories); map paper (Li'l Davis Designs); blue circle paper (American Crafts); vintage paper (Anna Griffin); script paper (Karen Foster Design); imagine sticker (NRN Design); travel sticker (Destination Scrapbook Designs); quote sticker (Wordsworth); definition sticker, hinges (Making Memories); letter stickers (Me & My Big Ideas); tag (DMD); transparency (Design Originals); alphabet stamp (Stampendous); metal embellishment (Scrapworks); adhesive (Therm O Web)

Enjoy Freely a Vast Horizon

ACCENT

Jenn combines multiple accent techniques using patterned paper for a border, photo mat and title letters. Layer a bottle-cap border with strips of blue and red patterned paper. Place green paper over red and secure a large photo mat. Create the title by printing the mirror image on the backside of patterned paper and cut out with a craft knife. Ink the edges of each letter and adhere to green paper. Print the script part of the title and journaling on a transparency and place over title and photo mat. Adhere the photo on top of the transparency and accent with painted metal embellishments.

Jenn Brookover, San Antonio, Texas

SUPPLIES: Bottle-cap paper (Design Originals); blue paper (Basic Grey); red paper (Sweetwater); green paper (Pixie Press); cream paper (Chatterbox); stamping inks (Clearsnap, Ranger, Stampin' Up!, Tsukineko); transparency (ACCO); metal accents (EK Success); acrylic paint (Making Memories)

TIP: *Use the pointed edge of a makeup sponge to ink inside the letters. This gives more control of the ink in the area of application.*

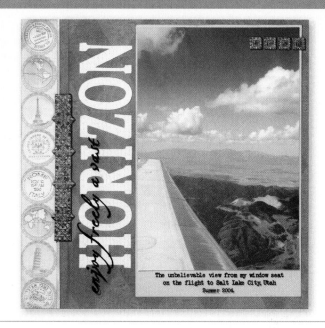

Vegas Escape

EMBELLISHMENT

Compile memorabilia and accents to create a 3-D embellishment on the page. Cut six equal sizes of patterned paper 4 x 4½", adhere wrong sides together with paper adhesive and rub the edges with ink. Punch small holes along sides to create the binding. Use jump rings and ribbon for the hinges of each page. Embellish with playing card paper, charms, watch face, rub-ons, metal accents and reduced images of memorabilia.

Jenn Brookover, San Antonio, Texas

SUPPLIES: Patterned paper (Paper Loft); diamond paper (7 Gypsies); playing card paper (Design Originals); letters (Mustard Moon); ink (Clearsnap); charms (Boxer Scrapbook Productions); metal accents, ribbon, jump rings, brads, paper tags, rub-ons (Making Memories); clock face (7 Gypsies); polka-dot and striped ribbon (May Arts); gingham ribbon (Offray); Modge Podge paper adhesive (Plaid); postcard sticker (EK Success); poker chip; staples; tickets

TIP: *"Test" the movement of the book on a scrapbook page by using a repositionable adhesive. Make sure the elements are visible as the book is opened in the desired order.*

Explore Hawaii

BACKGROUND

Themed paper creates a background for a bright woven mat. Create the page background by tearing the top off floral paper and layering on top of leaf paper. Create the photo and journaling mat by weaving ½" strips of green and pink papers. Use eyelets and paper ribbon to tie title around center of page. Print journaling on vellum and adhere to tags, attach to ribbon with jump ring. Stamp across top of woven paper.

Pam Klassen

Photos: Dawn Mabe, Lakewood, Colorado

SUPPLIES: Orange and green patterned papers (Frances Meyer); pink paper (Karen Foster Design); green cardstock (Bazzill); number stickers (Creative Imaginations); tags (Gartner Studios); stamp (Wordsworth); paper ribbon (Emagination Crafts); jump rings (Junkitz); adhesive (Therm O Web)

TIP: *When weaving paper, start from the center, adding strips on each side to keep the weave tight.*

A Trip to Visit My Brother

MONOCHROMATIC

Ink edges of monochromatic papers to add depth. Print bullet journaling on 8½ x 11" cardstock, ink the edges and accent with paper shapes and brads. Brush ink over selected words to highlight. Ink the edges of the photo before adhering to cardstock and mounting on the page. Stamp date and adhere in a fastener. Accent the page with a ribbon, attach with brads. To create the title, print the mirror image on the back of patterned paper and cut out.

Sue Thomas, Anoka, Minnesota

SUPPLIES: Background paper (Pebbles); plaid, crackle, checked papers (Daisy D's); travel text paper (Two Busy Moms); light brown cardstock (Bazzill); date stamp, brads (Making Memories); ink (Clearsnap); metal fastener (ACCO); ribbon

Santa Fe

CREATE YOUR OWN

Resist techniques add rich pattern and texture to this page design. Follow the steps below to create the patterned, textured cardstock. Cut newly designed patterned cardstock diagonally and trim off edges; layer with complementary-colored, textured cardstock over brown textured background. Machine stitch a zigzag pattern around the edges. Place ribbon through buckle rings and secure with eyelets set in the ribbon. Tie the two buckles together with green twill tape. Ink the edges of a double mat, adhere photo and place on the page.

Brandi Ginn

Photo: Sheila Michalski, Town and Country, Missouri

SUPPLIES: Cardstock (Bazzill); alphabet stamps (Hero Arts, Ma Vinci's Reliquary, Wordsworth); Versa Mark watermark ink, Versa Magic chalk ink (Tsukineko); extra thick embossing powder (Ranger); ribbon; buckles (7 Gypsies); twill tape (Creek Bank Creations)

TIP: *Heat the embossing powder from underneath the cardstock. This will allow the powder to melt evenly and each letter will be smooth and defined.*

1 Stamp words throughout textured cardstock using a watermark inkpad and various alphabet stamps.

2 Apply ultra thick embossing enamel and heat set.

3 Use a make up sponge to rub chalk in a circular motion over the entire surface of cardstock.

Yosemite

DOUBLE-SIDED

Layer and tear to reveal doubled-sided paper and showcase a special trip. Adhere a 6" strip of the blue double-sided paper on the right edge of the green background page. Cover completely with brown double-sided paper, laying stripe side down, adhere on the sides and bottom. Tear blue and brown papers down the center of page to reveal background paper. Mount photos and map in torn opening. Print journaling on transparency and adhere under photos. Add sticker title on torn paper.

Pam Klassen
Photos: Carolyn Foster, Reedley, California

SUPPLIES: Green patterned, blue circle papers (American Crafts); double-sided striped paper, letter stickers (SEI); adhesive (Therm O Web)

TIP: *Give sticker frames dimension by mounting on the layout with foam adhesive.*

Yellowstone

COORDINATING

Use coordinating papers layered across the page as photo and journaling mats. Starting in upper left corner, lay first strip across page. Ink edges of striped paper before adding a strip down page across first strip. Add green strip across bottom of page and striped paper last ending halfway up the page. Mat top photos on dark paper before adhering to strips. Print journaling and adhere on shorter strip. Cut small rectangles to mount sticker title. Use sticker frames and jute to mount date. Adhere preprinted tag to journaling strip with tack accents.

Pam Klassen
Photos: Michele Gerbrandt, Memory Makers

SUPPLIES: Coordinating patterned paper, tag (KI Memories); letter stickers (SEI, Wordsworth); frame sticker (K & Company); snaps (Chatterbox); adhesive (Therm O Web); jute

TIP: *Use minimal adhesive so that when stitching in place the needle will not become covered with glue.*

Portugal

ALTER

Give collage patterned papers a unique look by tearing and stitching them together. Follow the steps below to create collage borders. Cover the edge of collaged papers with orange twill tape. Mat photo on light orange cardstock and ink the edges. Create the title using various foam and rubber alphabet stamps with acrylic paint placed on pieces of canvas.

Brandi Ginn

Photos: Sheila Michalski, Town and Country, Missouri

SUPPLIES: Patterned paper (Deluxe Designs); chalk ink (Tsukineko); foam stamps, acrylic paint (Making Memories); rubber stamps (Ma Vinci's Reliquary); twill tape (Creek Bank Creations); Memory Tape Runner and Super Tape adhesives (Therm O Web)

1 Tear pieces of patterned paper in random shapes.

2 Arrange and layer on the cardstock.

3 Machine stitch the shapes in place following along the torn edge. Roll back the torn side for dimension.

Chapter THIRTEEN

Classic retro is back. From fonts, colors and patterns, the era of decades past is finding its way into our albums. Bold designs and color combinations you've never thought to use can be warm and inviting or bright and expressive. Using these papers doesn't have to be intimidating. Watch how we combine retro-style patterned papers successfully with pictures from both past and present.

Hair Do's and Don'ts

BACKGROUND

Use retro colors and patterns to create a classic look from the 60s. Cut top and bottom borders of brown patterned paper at angles. Using a homemade foam stamp (see page 61 for step-by-step instructions) and lavender acrylic paint, randomly stamp asterisk images on patterned paper and place on brown cardstock. Cover seams with ribbon and use die-cut letters for the title.

Brandi Ginn

Photos: Barbara Thompson, Aurora, Colorado

SUPPLIES: Patterned paper (Chatterbox); brown paper (Sassafras Lass); acrylic paint (Making Memories); spiral clip (Creative Impressions); die-cut letters (QuicKutz)

Circular Variation

Create a retro design using graphic pinks and browns accented with printed twill tape. Print the title on a transparency and adhere.

SUPPLIES: Patterned paper (Deluxe Designs); printed twill tape (7 Gypsies); transparency (Grafix)

Geometric Variation

Create the title by printing the mirror image on the back of green cardstock and cut out with a craft knife.

SUPPLIES: Patterned paper (SEI)

Sisters

ACCENT

Accent a page by hanging a floral journaling block. Print title and journaling on striped paper. Age edges of background paper, photo mat and striped journaling papers with inkpad. Mount journaling to floral paper. Use a craft knife to cut ⅝" horizontal slits on the tops and bottoms of mats. Starting at the top of photo frame, run ribbon behind frame, out the bottom, weaving through journaling block, back up behind it then to the top of photo frame to tie and secure. Cross ribbon across itself on journaling chain and secure to page with Zots adhesive.

Pam Klassen
Photo: Marjorie Klassen, Selma, California

SUPPLIES: Floral patterned paper (Anna Griffin); striped paper (Chatterbox); pale pink, blue, cream cardstocks (Bazzill); ink (Clearsnap); adhesive (Therm O Web); twill ribbon

Memory Pockets

EMBELLISHMENT

Fold a pocket to contain themed papers, photo and memorabilia. Cut a rectangle for pocket; score one end of paper following the steps below. Adhere papers together and slip into pocket. Add photo, feather and transparency. Pull ribbon from back through concho holes and tie in front. Print journaling on tag and add to pocket with a clothespin.

Pam Klassen
Photo: Pam Klassen & Lori Pope, Reedley, California

SUPPLIES: Background patterned paper (Reminiscence Papers); script paper (Design Originals); green paper (Anna Griffin); mulberry paper, tag (DMD); border sticker (Magenta); ribbon (Artchix Studio); conchos (Scrapworks); adhesive (Therm O Web); clothespin

Themed Variation

A themed paper style easily sets the tone to capture the look of an era.

SUPPLIES: Background paper (American Crafts); yellow paper, vellum (KI Memories); multi-patterned paper; number stickers (Karen Foster Design); ribbon (Artchix Sudio); conchos (Scrapworks); clip (7 Gypsies) adhesive (Therm O Web)

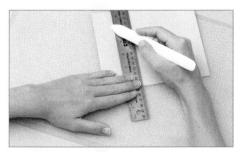

1 Cut rectangle 6 x 7½" and use bone folder to score 1½" from short end and fold over.

2 Press conchos through paper into soft mat on each side of folded end and secure. Punch through opening in concho with ⁵⁄₁₆" round hand punch.

3 Fill pocket with papers, photo and memorabilia, pull ribbon through concho holes and tie in front; clothespin journaling to page.

Swimming in the Seventies

BACKGROUND

Shannon chose bright retro papers and accents to create her design. Round the corners of the pictures with a corner punch, mat on black cardstock and place on the patterned paper background. To create the title, place letter stickers on coordinating patterned paper, mat on black cardstock and adhere vertically to the layout. Create a border along the bottom by using embroidery floss to stitch images on red paper that mirror those found in the patterned paper. Print journaling on a transparency and brush acrylic paint on the back before adhering to the page. Accent with a premade quote mounted on foam adhesive and a strip of blue cardstock.

Shannon Taylor, Bristol, Tennessee
Photos: Jon Burks

SUPPLIES: All patterned papers, sticker letters, premade accent (Arctic Frog); embroidery floss (DMC); transparency (Magic Scraps); acrylic paint (Delta); foam adhesive (Therm O Web)

Seventies Kids

MONOCHROMATIC

Keeping with the design of the patterned paper, Shannon rounded all the corners of each element used on her page. Use a corner punch to round all corners of patterned paper, journaling block and the picture. Frame patterned paper with solid cardstock and place the picture on the left side of the page. Accent the picture by placing a strip of solid paper through a buckle, wrap around each side and adhere in the back. Create the title by printing the mirror image on the back of teal cardstock and cut out with a craft knife. Add a glossy finish to the letters by using a liquid dimensional adhesive and allow to dry. Paint a piece of screen with acrylic paint and layer with the title letters. Print journaling on teal cardstock and adhere to the page. Cut graphic accents from coordinating paper with a craft knife and use to embellish the design.

Shannon Taylor, Bristol, Tennessee

SUPPLIES: Patterned paper (Two Busy Moms); buckle (Junkitz); liquid dimensional adhesive (JudiKins); metal mesh (Making Memories); adhesive (Therm O Web)

TIP: *If the decoupage causes the page to warp, use a warm iron on the back of the page to press it flat.*

Sasha

CREATE YOUR OWN

Collage a vintage background with torn paper strips of soft vintage prints. Paint white script paper with sheer color. Layer the background with two large strips of torn paper. Follow directions below to tear strips for the collage and adhere them to the layout. Cover center strip with small torn pieces, then space the torn strips vertically on each side of the center. Brush tea-dye over finished page. Print title and cut to place across page. Hand tint flowers in the photo. Mat the photo on cardstock and accent with buttons. Stamp date on tags.

Pam Klassen

Photo: Michele Gerbrandt, Memory Makers

SUPPLIES: Patterned paper backgrounds (Design Originals, EK Success, Rusty Pickle); script papers (7 Gypsies, Papers by Catherine); black cardstock (Bazzill); number stamps (Making Memories); buttons (Junkitz); photo color pen (SpotPen); Sheer Color gel medium, Decoupage, Tea Dye stain (Delta); paint (Plaid); adhesive (Therm O Web); tags

1 Follow directions to mix Sheer Color with red paint and paint white paper; let dry.

2 Tear strips of similar width papers along side of ruler.

3 Paint decoupage glue on paper backs and adhere to background page; let dry completely.

4 Paint completed page with tea-dye varnish; let dry.

First Kiss

DOUBLE-SIDED

Jenn pieced together patterned papers on brown cardstock to create the background of her page. Layer polka-dot ribbon along the bottom edge of patterned papers. Place an enlarged photo in the center of the page and adhere on three sides. Print the journaling in brown ink on white cardstock and place on a pullout element. Accent the element with polka-dot ribbon and metal embellishment; slide behind the photo. To create each square in the border, first cut a piece of patterned paper 2½" square. Cut a second piece of patterned paper 2½ x 5" and fold in half. Place the square inside the folded paper, roll back the open side, and secure with a decorative brad. Repeat three times using various patterned papers for each square. To create the title, print the mirror image on the back of white and brown cardstocks and cut out with a craft knife. Accent the name and date journaling with a metal bookplate.

Jenn Brookover, San Antonio, Texas

SUPPLIES: All patterned paper (SEI); brown and white cardstocks (Bazzill); ribbon (Li'l Davis Designs); metal swirl (Card Connection); decorative brads (Making Memories); solvent ink (Tsukineko); bookplate

TIP: *To create a simple detail, hold a solvent inkpad perpendicular to the edges of the picture and apply ink to each side.*

Wishes for My Sister

COORDINATING

Jenn combined retro papers with modern pictures to design a page for her sister. Cut light blue cardstock 7½" wide, lightly sand and layer with striped paper and brown cardstock; place in the center of patterned paper. Adhere cream ribbon along the bottom edge of blue cardstock. Create the top ribbon accent by threading brown ribbon through each side of a metal ring, wrap around the sides and secure in back. Flatten the back of an eyelet snap and adhere to ribbon with circle adhesive giving the appearance of a brad. Ink the edges of each picture and mount at angles on the page. Use alphabet stamps and brown ink to print journaling, date and a portion of the title. Use foam stamps and stamping ink to create the largest word in the title and accent with paper flowers, buttons and staples.

Jenn Brookover, San Antonio, Texas

SUPPLIES: Patterned paper, cream ribbon, snaps, foam stamps, date stamp, paper flowers (Making Memories); ink (Tsukineko); brown ribbon; ring (Li'l Davis Designs); alphabet stamps (EK Success, PSX Design); staples

TIP: *Add a subtle detail to word strips by holding the inkpad perpendicular to the paper and inking just the edges.*

High School Memories

ALTER

Alter patterned paper with transparencies and linen tape. Follow directions below to color two 12" lengths of linen tape. After positioning letter stickers on background paper, follow step 3 to adhere transparencies. Add sticker numbers, mat photo on script paper and adhere to page. Print title on tag and print a small photo to frame in concho and secure to tag. Thread tag and key onto ribbon; wrap and secure behind page.

Pam Klassen
Photo: Tammy Stegall, Reedley, California

SUPPLIES: Background patterned paper (Design Originals); script paper (7 Gypsies); transparencies (Artchix Studio, Carolee's Creations); linen tape (Lineco); tag (7 Gypsies); letter stickers (Me & My Big Ideas); number stickers (Pebbles); conchos (Scrapworks); metal key (Artchix Studio); adhesive (Therm O Web); ribbon

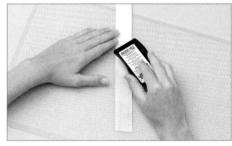

1 Rub linen tape with stamp pad to color, let dry.

2 Stamp linen tape with script stamp, let dry.

3 Position transparencies on background paper over sticker letters and secure in place by taping edges to page with linen tape.

Patterns

Use these reproducible project patterns to complete scrapbook pages featured in this book. Use a photocopier to enlarge patterns to the desired size needed to fit in your page layout.

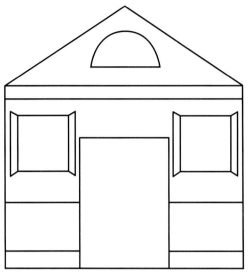

Page 33, Mother

Page 38, Saving Summer

Page 51, Rolled Holiday Tree & Pumpkin

Additional Instructions & Credits

COVER ART BLOOM AND GROW

Layer various patterned papers along the left side to create a border. Tear orange patterned paper at an angle and place in the upper right corner, layer with patterned paper. Mat photo on purple paper; accent with painted metal photo corners. Stamp gold cardstock with a script stamp, then use foam letters and paint to create the title. Accent the title by covering a slide mount with patterned paper and embellish with letter tiles and brads. Print journaling block on yellow cardstock; rubbing the edges with ink.

Brandi Ginn

SUPPLIES: Plaid, floral, purple patterned papers (Deluxe Designs); red dot paper, brads (Lasting Impressions); striped paper, photo corners, foam stamps, acrylic paint, black ribbon (Making Memories); orange paper (KI Memories); black-and-white floral paper (Chatterbox); green and yellow cardstocks (Bazzill); script stamp (Hero Arts); ink (Ranger); letter tiles (Junkitz); flower button (Doodlebug Designs); slide mount (Design Originals)

PAGE 6 SMILE GIRLS

Trim plaid paper and place on brown cardstock. Machine stitch a zigzag pattern along the right side of the page. Cut floral paper 5¼" wide, distress the edges with sandpaper and place over plaid paper. Mat photos on brown cardstock and adhere to library cards. Chalk the edges of library cards with brown chalk and accent with tabbed letters. Create part of the title using stencil letters rubbed with chalk. String letters on twine and place through rivets. To create word strip cut brown patterned paper to fit through a label maker and emboss the letters. Gently sand the top of the letters with sand paper to reveal the white core.

Brandi Ginn

SUPPLIES: Patterned papers (Chatterbox); brown and olive cardstocks (Bazzill); library cards, stencils, letters (Autumn Leaves); chalk (Deluxe Designs); foam adhesive (Therm O Web)

PAGE 6 JACQUELYN & AMANDA

Mount patterned paper background in center of page. Tear and cut complementary patterned paper strips and mount on page to frame center. Print journaling on transparency; adhere. Crop and mat photos; adhere. Freehand draw and cut out paper flowers; add glitter and adhere. Finish with metal corner accents.

Pam Klassen

SUPPLIES: Patterned papers (Anna Griffin, Chatterbox, Deluxe Designs, Design Originals, Pixie Press); glitter (Deco Art); metal corner accents (Making Memories)

PAGE 8 FAMILIES ARE A BLESSING

Cut strips of patterned paper in various widths and place them vertically on green cardstock. Create a border with brown ribbon and place across the bottom. Mat photos on patterned paper and adhere to the page. Create the title on cardstock, rub the edges with chalk and accent the design with square brads.

Brandi Ginn, Photos: Robert Woods, Layton, Utah

SUPPLIES: Script paper (Rusty Pickle); letter paper, chalk (Deluxe Designs); yellow and red patterned paper (Carolee's Creations); brads (Making Memories); ribbon

PAGE 8 LITTLE ARTIST

Layer green and blue papers and place on purple cardstock. Mat one photo on blue cardstock. Create a square frame and layer over the picture to frame the subject. Create the title with letter stickers and accent with purple buttons.

Brandi Ginn, Photos: Staci Langford, Erie, Colorado

SUPPLIES: Patterned paper, buttons (Lasting Impressions); cardstock (Bazzill); letter stickers (Deluxe Designs); framed letter stickers (Wordsworth)

PAGE 8 MONTGOMERY

Tear a large piece of patterned paper and layer on pink paper. Add strips of yellow paper at angles along the bottom and use foam stamps and paint to create the title. Place various patterned papers around a frame and place over the picture. Accent with flower tiles embellished with rub-on letters.

Brandi Ginn, Photo: Richard Komas of Tiny Studio, Kenosha, Wisconsin

SUPPLIES: Letter paper (Deluxe Designs); yellow, red floral papers (KI Memories); pink circle paper (Scrapbook Wizard); flower tiles (Little Black Dress Designs); rub-on letters, foam stamps, stencil, paint (Making Memories); charm (Card Connection); ribbon

PAGE 9 DAD

Cut red monochromatic papers in various sizes and place on black cardstock to create the background. Frame the pictures on red cardstock and paint the edges with black paint. Paint the outside of the stencils red and the edges black. Add black to the painted red letters using a stipple brush. Place ribbons along the side and bottom edges creating a border.

Brandi Ginn

SUPPLIES: Patterned paper (Memories Complete); script paper (7 Gypsies); stencils, photo anchors, ribbon, ribbon charm, paint (Making Memories)

PAGE 9 DADDY'S GIRLS

High-Value Variation

Cut a large piece of patterned paper and layer at an angle on the background. Mat photos on white cardstock and paint the edges with blue paint. Print the title on white cardstock and use die-cut letters for the journaling. Embellish photos and title with metal accents and create a border along the bottom with ribbon and twill tape.

Brandi Ginn

SUPPLIES: Patterned paper (All My Memories); metal accents (Making Memories); letters (Foofala); twill tape (Creek Bank Creations); ribbon (Offray)

Low-Value Variation

Cut a large piece of patterned paper and layer at an angle on the background. Place the photos on the design and accent with metal photo anchors attached with brads. Print the title and journaling on cardstock and embellish with metal accents. Create the border along the bottom using ribbon and accent with a black button.

Brandi Ginn

SUPPLIES: Patterned paper (Paper Patch); brads (Lasting Impressions); metal accents, button (Making Memories); black ribbon (Offray); striped ribbon

PAGE 10 SWEET ATTITUDE

Place circle patterned paper on pink cardstock; at the seam place a strip of white cardstock. Layer borders of yellow patterned paper on the top and bottom of the page. Adhere two strips of ribbon along the bottom border. Cover portions of the yellow paper with white cardstock and stamp the title using black paint, allowing the letters to extend beyond the cardstock. Mat photos on yellow paper and accent with silk flowers attached with pink brads.

Brandi Ginn

SUPPLIES: Patterned paper (KI Memories); foam stamps, flowers, brads, and paint (Making Memories); ribbon

PAGE 10 YOU BRING ME JOY

Trim and layer two papers across the center of green background so edges from lower pages show. Cut frame from script paper, tearing one end. Mount onto page over floral paper. Adhere linen tape across center of page and stamp title, changing color and framing final word. Add name with rub-on letters. Using a craft knife, cut small slits in background paper to mount corners of the photo.

Pam Klassen; Photo: Kelli Noto, Centennial, Colorado

SUPPLIES: Striped, polka-dot, floral patterned papers (Treehouse Designs); text paper (Karen Foster Design); rub on letters (Autumn Leaves); letter stamps (PSX Design); ribbon (Artchix Studios); metal frame (Pebbles); adhesive (Therm O Web)

PAGE 11 SWEET, SMILES, SECRETS

Place white flower paper on green patterned paper. Mat red patterned paper on green cardstock and adhere to white flower paper. Adhere green ribbon along the bottom and place photos on the page. Use rub-on letters in the empty space of the photos to act as journaling. Wrap patterned paper around the square portion of the letter stencil. Paint the letter and place within the stencil; adhere to the page.

Brandi Ginn

SUPPLIES: Patterned paper (Chatterbox); stencil, rub-ons (Making Memories); ribbon

PAGE 11 YOU GIVE ME LAUGHTER

Cut a strip of argyle paper to cover the top of floral paper. Tear off the bottom of floral paper and layer on top of swirl paper. Use inks to color linen tape, let dry. Use one strip to cover seam between top papers, and remaining tape to cover frame. Print oversized letter and cut out; die cut the remaining letters of the name. Stamp title and adhere to frame with brads. Print text on transparency and paint reverse side. Embellish with buttons.

Pam Klassen; Photo: Ryan Watamura, Reedley, California

SUPPLIES: Floral patterned paper (Colors by Design); swirl paper (Treehouse Designs); argyle paper (Frances Meyer); frame (Design Originals); alphabet stamps (Making Memories); die-cut letters (Quic-Kutz); paint (Plaid); buttons (Junkitz); adhesive (Therm O Web)

PAGE 12 PRESERVING OUR PAST

Cut pink script paper to run vertically across cardstock background. Cut down paisley and striped papers. Use inkpad to color the edges of all patterned papers. Adhere paisley paper to script page, using a zigzag stitch on two edges. Print quote on bottom of striped paper, adhere to paisley with a zigzag stitch on two edges. Stamp name and date. Wrap ribbons around back and secure ends to layout with decorative brads.

Pam Klassen

SUPPLIES: Script paper, floral paper (Rusty Pickle); striped paper (Sandylion); yellow cardstock (Bazzill); alphabet stamps (Ma Vinci's Reliquary); ink (Clearsnap); decorative brads (Making Memories); adhesive (Therm O Web); ribbon

PAGE 12 WAYNE

Machine stitch a wide strip of blue paper to background along one edge. Tear two narrow strips of patterned paper the length of the page. Roll torn edges and brush with inkpad, layer and adhere next to large blue strip. Cover the seam with ribbon and adhere on the back. Cover stencil with paper, cutting letter out with craft knife. Layer Maruyana under letter and attach to layout with foam adhesive. Layer brown script paper on black cardstock and cut a large circle in the center to frame photo. Wrap lower frame with ribbon to hold the title and attach to the layout with foam adhesive. Print quote on transparency and mount on papers using photo clips.

Pam Klassen

SUPPLIES: Music paper (Rusty Pickle); script paper (K & Company); blue vintage papers (Anna Griffin); brown script papers (Papers by Catherine); black cardstock (Bazzill); stencil letter (Ma Vinci's Reliquary); snaps (Chatterbox); metal clips (Making Memories); foam adhesive and adhesive (Therm O Web); ribbon

Source Guide

The following companies manufacture products featured in this book. Please check your local retailers to find these materials, or go to a company's Web site for the latest product. In addition, we have made every attempt to properly credit the items mentioned in this book. We apologize to any company that we have listed incorrectly, and we would appreciate hearing from you.

7 Gypsies
(800) 588-6707
www.7gypsies.com
ACCO Brands
(800) 989-4923
www.acco.com
Alextamping
(209) 533-1834
www.alextamping.com
All My Memories
(888) 553-1998
www.allmymemories.com
All Night Media (see Plaid Enterprises)
American Crafts
(801) 226-0747
www.americancrafts.com
American Tag Co.
(800) 223-3956
www.americantag.net
AMPAD® (American Pad & Paper, LLC)
(800) 426-1368
www.ampad.com
Anna Griffin, Inc.
(wholesale only)
(888) 817-8170
www.annagriffin.com
Arctic Frog
(479) 636-FROG
www.arcticfrog.com

ARTchix Studio
(250) 370-9985
www.artchixstudio.com
Autumn Leaves (wholesale only)
(800) 588-6707
www.autumnleaves.com
Avery Dennison Corporation
(800) GO-AVERY
www.avery.com
Basic Grey™
(801) 451-6006
www.basicgrey.com
Bazzill Basics Paper
(480) 558-8557
www.bazzillbasics.com
Beacon Adhesives, Inc.
(914) 699-3400
www.beaconcreates.com
Bisous
(905) 502-7209
www.bisous.biz
Bo-Bunny Press
(801) 771-4010
www.bobunny.com
Boxer Scrapbook Productions
(888) 625-6255
www.boxerscrapbooks.com
Brother Sister Design Studio—see Hobby Lobby
Canson®, Inc.
(800) 628-9283
www.canson-us.com
Card Connection—see Michaels
Carolee's Creations®
(435) 563-1100
www.ccpaper.com
Chatterbox, Inc.
(208) 939-9133
www.chatterboxinc.com
Clearsnap, Inc.
(800) 448-4862
www.clearsnap.com
Colorbök™, Inc.
(800) 366-4660
www.colorbok.com
Colors by Design
(800) 832-8436
www.colorsbydesign.com
Craf-T Products
(507) 235-3996
www.craf-tproducts.com
Crafter's Workshop, The
(877) CRAFTER
www.thecraftersworkshop.com
Creative Imaginations
(800) 942-6487
www.cigift.com
Creative Impressions Rubber Stamps, Inc.
(719) 596-4860
www.creativeimpressions.com
Creek Bank Creations, Inc.
(217) 427-5980
www.creekbankcreations.com
Crop In Style
(888) 700-2202
www.cropinstyle.com
Cropper Hopper™/Advantus Corporation
(800) 826-8806
www.cropperhopper.com
C-Thru® Ruler Company, The
(800) 243-8419
www.cthruruler.com
Daisy D's Paper Company
(888) 601-8955
www.daisydspaper.com
DecoArt™, Inc.
(800) 367-3047
www.decoart.com
Delta Technical Coatings, Inc.
(800) 423-4135
www.deltacrafts.com
Deluxe Designs
(480) 205-9210
www.deluxedesigns.com
Design Originals
(800) 877-0067
www.d-originals.com

Destination™ Scrapbook Designs
(866) 806-7826
www.destinationstickers.com
Diane's Daughters®
(801) 621-8392
www.dianesdaughters.com
DMC Corp.
(973) 589-0606
www.dmc.com
DMD Industries, Inc.
(800) 805-9890
www.dmdind.com
Doodlebug Design™ Inc.
(801) 966-9952
www.doodlebugdesigninc.com
Dover Publications, Inc.
(800) 223-3130
www.doverpublications.com
Dymo
www.dymo.com
EK Success™, Ltd.
(800) 524-1349
www.eksuccess.com
Emagination Crafts, Inc.
(630) 833-9521
www.emaginationcrafts.com
FoofaLa
(402) 758-0863
www.foofala.com
Frances Meyer
(413) 584-5446
www.francesmeyer.com
Gartner Studios, Inc.
www.uprint.com
Grafix® Graphic Art Systems, Inc.
(800) 447-2349
www.grafixarts.com
Happy Hammer, The
(303) 690-3883
www.thehappyhammer.com
Heidi Grace Designs
(866) 89-HEIDI
www.heidigrace.com
Hero Arts® Rubber Stamps, Inc.
(800) 822-4376
www.heroarts.com
Hirschberg Schutz & Co., Inc.
(800) 221-8640
Hobby Lobby Stores, Inc.
www.hobbylobby.com
Hot Off The Press, Inc.
(800) 227-9595
www.paperpizazz.com
Inkadinkado® Rubber Stamps
(800) 888-4652
www.inkadinkado.com
JewelCraft LLC
(201) 223-0804
www.jewelcraft.biz
Jo-Ann Fabric & Crafts
(888) 739-4120
www.joann.com
JudiKins
(310) 515-1115
www.judikins.com
Junkitz™
(732) 792-1108
www.junkitz.com
K & Company
(888) 244-2083
www.kandcompany.com
Karen Foster Design
(801) 451-9779
www.karenfosterdesign.com
Keeping Memories Alive™
(800) 419-4949
www.scrapbooks.com
KI Memories
(972) 243-5595
www.kimemories.com
Krylon®
(216) 566-200
www.krylon.com

Lasting Impressions for Paper, Inc.
(801) 298-1979
www.lastingimpressions.com
Li'l Davis Designs
(949) 838-0344
www.lildavisdesigns.com
Lineco, Inc.
(800) 322-7775
www.lineco.com
Little Black Dress Designs
(360) 894-8844
www.littleblackdressdesigns.com
Ma Vinci's Reliquary
www.crafts.dm.net/mall/reliquary/
Magenta Rubber Stamps
(800) 565-5254
www.magentastyle.com
Magic Mesh
(651) 345-6374
www.magicmesh.com
Magic Scraps™
(972) 238-1838
www.magicscraps.com
Magnetic Poetry®
(800) 370-7697
www.magneticpoetry.com
Making Memories
(800) 286-5263
www.makingmemories.com
May Arts
(800) 442-3950
www.mayarts.com
me & my BiG ideas®
(949) 883-2065
www.meandmybigideas.com
Memories Complete™, LLC
(866) 966-6365
www.memoriescomplete.com
Michaels® Arts & Crafts
(800) 642-4235
www.michaels.com
Microsoft Corporation
www.microsoft.com
Moto Photo
(800) 454-6686
www.motophoto.com
Mustard Moon™
(408) 299-8542
www.mustardmoon.com
NRN Designs
(800) 421-6958
www.nrndesigns.com
Nunn Design
(360) 379-3557
www.nunndesign.com
Offray
www.offray.com
Paper Adventures®
(800) 727-0699
www.paperadventures.com
Paper Fever, Inc.
(800) 477-0902
www.paperfever.com
Paper Loft, The
(801) 254-1961
www.paperloft.com
Paper Patch®, The
(800) 397-2737
www.paperpatch.com
Papers by Catherine
(713) 723-3334
www.papersbycatherine.com
Pebbles Inc.
(801) 224-1857
www.pebblesinc.com
Pixie Press
(800) 834-2883
www.pixiepress.com
Plaid Enterprises, Inc.
(800) 842-4197
www.plaidonline.com
PrintWorks
(800) 854-6558
www.printworks.com

Provo Craft®
(888) 577-3545
www.provocraft.com
PSX Design™
(800) 782-6748
www.psxdesign.com
QuicKutz
(801) 765-1144
www.quickutz.com
Ranger Industries, Inc.
(800) 244-2211
www.rangerink.com
Reminiscence Papers
(503) 246-9681
www.reminiscencepapers.com
Rubber Stampede
(800) 423-4135
www.deltacrafts.com
Rusty Pickle
(801) 272-2280
www.rustypickle.com
Sandylion Sticker Designs
(800) 387-4215
www.sandylion.com
Sassafras Lass
(801) 269-1331
www.sassafraslass.com
Scrap Ease®
(800) 272-3874
www.whatsnewltd.com
Scrapbook Wizard™, The
(435) 752-7555
www.scrapbookwizard.com
Scrapworks, LLC
(801) 363-1010
www.scrapworks.com
Scrapyard 329
(775) 829-1118
www.scrapyard329.com
SEI, Inc.
(800) 333-3279
www.shopsei.com
Spotpen—no contact information
Springs Industries, Inc.
(888) 926-7888
www.springs.com
Stamp In The Hand Co., A
(310) 884-9700
www.astampinthehand.com
Stampendous!®
(800) 869-0474
www.stampendous.com
Stampin' Up!®
(800) 782-6787
www.stampinup.com
Suze Weinberg Design Studio
(732) 761-2400
www.schmoozewithsuze.com
Sweetwater
(800) 359-3094
www.sweetwaterscrapbook.com
Therm O Web, Inc.
(800) 323-0799
www.thermoweb.com
Tin Tiques—no contact information
Treehouse Designs
(501) 372-1109
www.treehouse-designs.com
Tsukineko®, Inc.
(800) 769-6633
www.tsukineko.com
Two Busy Moms—see Deluxe Designs
USArtQuest, Inc.
(517) 522-6225
www.usartquest.com
Wamsutta—see Springs Industries, Inc.
Wordsworth
(719) 282-3495
www.wordsworthstamps.com
Wübie Prints
(888) 256-0107
www.wubieprints.com

About the Authors

BRANDI GINN

As the only granddaughter of a professional photographer, Brandi was introduced to photography at an early age. She obtained her first SLR camera in a photography contest while competing for Miss Teen USA in Biloxi, Mississippi. This camera launched her interest in taking pictures for herself and has evolved her scrapbooking skills. Since being chosen as one of the original Memory Makers Masters, she has taught at various shows for Therm O Web and Deluxe Designs. She's also worked closely with Michele Gerbrandt, creating much of the artwork used in her Home Shopping Network and other television appearances. Brandi lives in Lafayette, Colorado, with her husband, Nathan, and daughters Alexa and Brinley. One week after finishing this book she gave birth to their third daughter, Natalie.

PAM KLASSEN

As a versatile scrapbook designer and artist, Pam has always been inspired by artistic color and patterns. Since her six years as craft editor for *Memory Makers* magazine, Pam has been continuously trying new techniques and designs. From creating magazine covers and artwork, she went on to develop products, demonstrate at trade shows and teach classes. With her second book in publication and many years of trial and error using patterned paper, she is qualified to teach others her tips, techniques and inspiration for using patterned paper to its best advantage. Pam is a busy mother of two girls, Amanda and Jacquelyn, and wife to Tony. Living in Reedley, California, she plans on continuing the privilege of developing inspiring ideas to share with readers. *A Passion for Patterned Paper* is Pam's second Memory Makers book. Her first book, *Memory Makers Making Gift Albums in a Snap*, is enjoying popularity and success.

Index

A

About the Authors 95
Additional Instructions & Credits 92-93
Accent Patterned Paper Ideas 15, 21, 27, 33, 39, 45, 51, 57, 63, 69, 75, 81, 87
Altered Patterned Paper Ideas 19, 25, 31, 37, 43, 49, 55, 61, 67, 73, 79, 85, 91

B

Baby 14-19
Background Patterned Paper Ideas 28, 16, 22, 34, 40, 46, 52, 58, 64, 70, 76, 82, 88
Birthday 20-25

C

Children 26-31
Color 8, 9
Coordinating Patterned Paper Ideas 36, 18, 24, 30, 42, 48, 54, 60, 66, 72, 76, 84, 90
Create Your Own Patterned Paper 17, 23, 29, 35, 41, 47, 53, 59, 65, 71, 77, 83, 89

D

Dedication 3
Double-Sided Patterned Paper Ideas 24, 42, 66, 84, 90

E

Embellishments Created With Patterned Paper 15, 21, 27, 33, 39, 45, 51, 57, 63, 69, 75, 81, 87

F

Fabric As Patterned Paper 36, 54
Feminine 32-37
Florals 10

G

Geometrics 10
Graphic-Design Ideas 38-4
Gutsy Color Combination 60

H

Heritage 44-49
Holidays & Seasons 50-55

I

Inspiration For Patterned Paper Selection 18, 30, 72, 78
Introduction 7

M

Masculine Ideas 56-61
Mixing & Matching Various Scales 11
Monochromatic Color 9
Monochromatic Patterned Paper Pages 16, 22, 28, 34, 40, 46, 52, 58, 64, 70, 78, 82, 88

N

Nature 62-67

P

Pattern 10
Patterns 92
Placement 12

S

Scale 11
School/Sports 68-73
Sentiments 74-79
Storage & Organization 13
Sources 92-93

T

Table of Contents 4-5
Tips 15, 16, 17, 18, 19, 23, 25, 28, 30, 33, 34, 36, 37, 42, 43, 46, 48, 49, 51, 55, 58, 59, 60, 63, 65, 66, 67, 71, 75, 77, 79, 81, 82, 83, 84, 85, 89, 90
Travel 80-85

V

Value 9
Vintage & Retro 86-91

W

Warm & Cool Colors 8